Inside Amazon

My Story

Gisela Hausmann

www.GiselaHausmann.com

Educ-Easy Books • Greenville, SC

***

***

Educ-Easy Books
POB 6366
Greenville, SC 29606
www.GiselaHausmann.com

***

Editor: Annie Verner-Hausmann

Photographer: Janet Boschker, NorthLight Photography Charlotte, NC

Cover Design: EbookLaunch

Ebook Formatting: EbookLaunch

ISBN 978-1-7324211-9-6

*

CONTENTS

FOREWORD

I am not an undercover reporter who wanted to snoop around and look for problems with Amazon's operations.

In fact, I used to be one of Jeff Bezos' and Amazon's greatest fans. Since I published five books about Amazon's review platform, reporters on two continents and thousands of indie authors can vouch for this truth. I also served as an Amazon top reviewer from 2014 to 2018 (best ranking #2,756) and I am a subscriber of *The Washington Post*.

Because I published five books about Amazon's review platform, I also believed that I would never write a book about Amazon again; in the past, I lost time and money on becoming an expert on Amazon's review platform. Since the company kept changing their modus operandi, I could never enjoy the fruits of my labor but had to update my books every year.

In 2019, I began working at Amazon Logistics because besides being an author I am also a transportation professional. Hence, I thought that working for one of the fastest-growing last-mile delivery logistics companies in the United States with a reputation for being highly efficient was a great idea.

This is my story.

However, it is not the complete story. Since I stopped working for Amazon only in December 2020, the company's non-disclosure agreement keeps me from telling everything I experienced. Missing are the stories of one employee getting fired for the wrong reason, an ill-designed light rod system, an instructional video that described a work process incorrectly, and of a workflow pattern that could have been designed much better (for the workers).

Then again, in their non-disclosure agreement Amazon states that non-supervisory employees are free to talk about their own or their coworkers' wages, hours, or working conditions. Also: obviously, information which has been "revealed/disclosed" before can never be protected by a non-disclosure agreement. (This book's addendum includes links to all references, sorted by topic.)

If George Orwell was right when he said that good writing is like a windowpane, you might find this story fascinating.

Here's to our stories!

Gisela Hausmann

My Story

- 1 -

In fall 1997 I decided that I wanted to write and self-publish a book, specifically – an alphabet book for early learners. Most of my friends reacted with surprise or even horror.

"A book? Are you crazy? It's probably easier to win the lottery than self-publish a book successfully. And, how are you going to get it into bookstores? They work with distributors only and getting one of them to sign you on will not be easy."

Of course, they were right, but I had discovered a solution to my and every self-publishing author's biggest problem: an Internet bookstore named Amazon.com.

Founded in 1995, Amazon was the brainchild of an entrepreneur named Jeff Bezos whose apparent goal was to disrupt superstore-chain Barnes & Noble's victory lap.

Barnes & Noble had acquired B. Dalton's 797 bookstores in 1986 and Doubleday Books' 40 bookstores in 1990, thereby effectively creating a bookselling superstore chain, which, in turn, lead to the decline of local, independent bookstores. Eventually, this story would become the backdrop of the movie *You've Got Mail*.

As a second side effect, Barnes & Noble's power grab of the industry also made self-publishing authors' lives harder. Whereas most independent bookstores accepted indie authors' books on consignment, Barnes & Noble's bookstores had vendor and product compliance requirements most independent authors could not meet.

And, then came Jeff Bezos.

His Internet bookstore operated with a radical, new concept. Instead of bothering with a complicated or time-consuming vetting process they accepted and distributed everybody's books. As soon as I read that, I sensed that the discriminating world of publishing and bookselling was about to be turned upside down.

Having self-published two books in my birth country Austria, I knew that authors had many options for creating, publishing, and marketing their books by themselves. Even aspiring authors who didn't want to get involved with the technical side of producing a book could hire a vanity publisher, some of whom did a fine job of printing books.

Authors could also market their books for next to nothing by doing author's readings in coffee houses, parks, and even bars. In reality, self-publishing authors' only insurmountable problem was answering the one question that really decided their book's fate – "And, where is your book available?"

As with all matters of marketing, branding, and sales the ideal response was a one-word answer every person would remember. Like, "At Amazon.com."

- 2 -

My alphabet book's concept was new and different too. Instead of presenting visual associations from a specific theme, like the names of toys or dinosaurs, my book was going to show pictures of items and action words that looked like the first letter of the words. For example, the capital letter "I" was represented by the associate words "I am here." The accompanying picture showed a young hedgehog responding to a roll call by raising his arm, which made the arm look like a capital "I." Educators and parents could use my book's pictures to teach the shapes and sounds of the letters using visual, auditory, and kinesthetic processes.

I was sure that the fact that my concept idea was different from the typical alphabet books would help me in getting book reviews in educators' magazines. Additionally, I would try to introduce the book in online teachers' chatrooms, which were quite in vogue in the late nineties.

And, if educators asked me, "Where is your book available?" I'd say "Nationwide at Amazon.com."

I spent the entire spring of 1998 selecting my associative words and working with my illustrator. Ozzie Pardillo was a very talented student at an arts college in Miami. He was willing to do exceptional work for relatively little money as he was close to graduation. What really mattered to Ozzie was the fact that I was going to print and publish his work even before he graduated. And, that I promised him that I would list him as my book's illustrator on Amazon, for everyone to see. He knew this would help him to land a dream job.

Next, I hired a printer. While they printed and bound my books, I opened a vendor's account at Amazon.

In the summer of 1998, Amazon was not the well-oiled sales machine it is today. They did not even have a phone number one could call. Every step of the process had to be handled via email; typically, Amazon's replies took two days. Because I published a picture book I was given the opportunity to sign up for the "Look into the Book"-feature. I ordered three scans at a copy store which the employee saved on a floppy disc so I could email them to Amazon. It took about two weeks until the images went live. Meanwhile Amazon ordered two copies of my book to put them in stock.

After that was done, I worked on my local marketing campaign. At the time I lived on the island of Key Largo about one-and-a-half hours south of Miami quite far from the next Barnes & Noble superstore. Key Largo was home to four independent bookstores that catered to the needs of locals and tourists who were looking for a captivating beach read. All four bookstore owners accepted my book for consignment; two of them even asked me to do a book signing sometime soon. Best of all, one bookstore owner asked me if I'd be interested to do guest speaker appearances at the school bookfairs she held at some private Miami schools every fall.

In the following two weeks I visited every independent bookstore and toy store in the Florida Keys, all the way south to Key West. I also approached all local newspapers including *The Miami Herald* and all of them agreed to feature my upcoming release. Soon everything was set for my book launch at the beginning of the new school year 1998/99.

It went amazing. *The Miami Herald* featured an article with a huge picture of me and my book on title page B1 of *The Miami Herald's* Keys edition – on the first day of school. When I dropped off my kids at the elementary school it seemed as if the whole town knew about it. Even people I didn't even know congratulated me as if I was already a bestselling author. The same week the other Florida Keys newspapers also published their articles and I sold many books.

The following week I used the articles to put together an impressive-looking press release and sent review copies to various educators' magazines. Since I knew it'd be at least four to five weeks until I'd hear from them, I turned my attention to the online teachers' chatrooms. There, I struck up conversations with many kindergarten teachers.

Alas, not one of them bought my book on Amazon.

I was frantic.

Had I misjudged the opportunities the new online bookstore offered?

My ever-supportive husband straightened me out. "Gisela, you know your stuff when it comes to talking to reporters or writing press releases, but you are new to this Internet thing. Everything's a learning process and nothing's all easy." Of course, he was right.

- 3 -

How could I find the solution to a problem of which I didn't know anything? I decided to write down everything I knew about book marketing. My own experiences of helping my husband create and market two expensive coffee-table books weren't useful because we never sold them in bookstores. Florian was an aerial photographer who took aerial pictures of Austrian companies' headquarters and factories for more than fifteen years. Therefore, he had a mailing list of Austrian Fortune 100 CEOs who were willing to spend real money on aerial portraits. And, he knew most of them personally. Not surprisingly, they were also interested in buying larger quantities of our gorgeous coffee-table books because they could use them as exceptional gifts for their business partners.

Among my friends whose work had been published by traditional publishers was Austrian scientist Rupert Riedl, bestselling author of more than half-a-dozen books. One time, after one of his books was released, I asked him how sales were going. He told me he wouldn't know for a while because he received that information only at the end of every quarter, which was the way things worked when phones and fax machines were the main tools of business communication.

Rupert also explained the system's shortfall for authors. Though he was a frequent guest on Austrian and German TV he had no way of finding out if the one or other appearance led to notable sales because bookstores didn't disclose sales numbers on the days he would have liked to see them.

But – Amazon did. Suddenly realizing my enormous advantage gave me pause. It was also the first clue that led me to understand that Jeff Bezos' business concept was going to make him very, very rich.

In the past, authors had to fly blind. They had no way of knowing if their PR activities worked out, or not. But working with Amazon would be different. Because they gave their vendors the data they needed. All I needed to do was to change the various elements of my marketing strategy until I learned what worked and what didn't.

Today, every Amazon author and vendor understands this concept, but in the late nineties it was mind boggling.

Feeling empowered by the fact that I could do what Rupert could never do I reexamined my comments in the chatrooms – again. Still, I couldn't find the reason for not even one kindergarten teacher buying a copy of my book. My conversations had been light and pleasant and never once had I been pushy and asked for the sale. Only when the educators asked where they could buy my book I replied, "Nationwide at Amazon.com, the Internet bookstore."

Why had none of them purchased a copy? Though most teachers aren't rich, surely all of them had a credit card.

Maybe, there was a problem with my Amazon book page?

I pulled up two browser windows and compared my Amazon book page side-by-side with that of an Amazon bestseller. What did this other book page have that mine didn't have?

A sales rank and – book reviews!

That was it! I needed to get book reviews.

Little did I guess that seventeen years later I'd be one of the nation's foremost experts on getting reviews on Amazon, and that a reporter from Bloomberg would visit me in person to interview me and learn my insights. For the moment I just did what probably every author in my situation would have done – I decided to cheat and ask my friends to post reviews.

Obviously, there was no other way. Since all sales had taken place at brick-and-mortar bookstores, I did not know the buyers unless they identified themselves.

In 1998, Amazon did not have any rules against "cheating." In fact, pondering the issue, I even came to the opinion that Jeff Bezos hoped that authors would cheat. Inevitably, every author who asked their friends to review their book served as an unpaid PR person for Bezos' new store because while asking for a review the authors also introduced Amazon to their friends. Word of mouth is and has always been the best advertising.

Hoping to solve this issue quickly I called my best friend. We met two years earlier when our sons became best friends in preschool. She also owned a home computer which was not the norm at the time.

"Hey, it's Gisela, can I ask you a favor?"

I explained and she listened.

"But I have never written a book review and it's been fifteen years since I wrote my last book report."

"Haha... No, you misunderstood me. I am not asking for a book report. A few lines will do. Maybe you could write how your son liked my *Obvious Letters*. Amazon's only requirement is that the review is longer than twenty words. It doesn't even matter if you ever purchased a book at Amazon."

"But, Gisela, I have to write something really good. The whole world will be able to read my words."

Right. Focused only on my agenda I had not even considered the bigger scope of things. "I think you are overestimating the task. It's a kids' book, not a Pulitzer prize winner."

She replied that she'd work on it.

An hour later I checked my Amazon book page. Nothing. No review. I looked again in the evening. Still nothing.

It was then that I realized that though I had prepared my book launch meticulously, I forgot to ask my friends to post reviews on launch day or soon afterwards. Considering that I studied film and mass media, it was quite embarrassing.

- 4 -

In fact, as a student of film and mass media I believed that Amazon's invitation to readers to post their opinions was pure genius. In the long run, the reviews' advertisement value would be priceless.

Most people trusted real people's opinions more than celebrities' or insiders' opinions because regular people aren't getting paid big bucks for sharing their thoughts about a product. I learned this when I worked as a director's assistant and production manager shooting commercials in Austria. At the time, I worked with quite a few real housewives who starred in commercials explaining how this or that personal care product, detergent, and even one margarine spread improved their and their family's lives.

All advertising industry professionals agreed that commercials with real people who could relate the product message honestly and authentically received the highest credibility ratings.

I guessed it'd be the same with book reviews. Readers would trust a review penned by Jane or Joe Doe more than the review of a critic who might know the author personally and love 'em or hate 'em.

I also believed that if my guess turned out to be true, Jeff Bezos' way of harnessing the advertisement value of real people's opinions – for free – would be the biggest marketing coup of this and the next decade.

But, like all good things in life, readers' reviews were hard to come by.

Because the concept of readers posting their thoughts was so new and radical, apparently, people were intimidated by the idea that somebody invited them to share their opinions.

If there was any consolation for me, it was that even books of bestselling authors did not amass reviews quickly. In early September, *Harry Potter and the Sorcerer's Stone* was released in the United States. It had a release like few other children's books because *Harry Potter* was already a bestseller in the United Kingdom. Yet, it took seventy days until a first review was posted on Amazon.

One reviewer wrote that they bought the book on the advice of a clerk at a children's bookstore. The reviewer also stated that their son read most of *Harry Potter* all by himself, because he was so excited about the story.

This review was priceless. In my mind I could see how it spoke to every parent in a much more relatable way than even the best review from a critic who would not dare mention that not every child enjoys reading.

A teenage reviewer explained that he loved the descriptions of Harry Potter's sport Quidditch and that he wished that it was a real sport because it was a "mix of sorcery and basketball." Though all teenagers and maybe even their parents understood the meaning of these words no critic would ever describe *Harry Potter* this way.

To me, these reviews illustrated why readers' reviews can be superior to that of experts' critiques. Readers' reviews described books using words that spoke to other readers. I was certain that the two comments sold a lot of books. Even more amazing was the fact that this type of perfect advertisement cost Amazon not even a penny (except for creating the review platform).

Unfortunately, my book did not garner such great reviews and I knew why. Since I asked for them, subconsciously, my friends were reminded of long-ago school days. The best reviews came from people who spontaneously shared what moved them, like the parent who was excited to "tell the world" that their child read *Harry Potter* by himself.

This realization left me wondering how Amazon planned to attract large numbers of this kind of review writers when they would receive nothing in return. Maybe at the time Jeff Bezos didn't even know it himself.

- 5 -

Four weeks later, the bookstore owner who wanted me to hold educational talks at her school bookfairs invited me to the opening of the first of the six events she held every year. The location was a Jewish school in Miami. Though I was a bit nervous the event went very well. Almost every parent purchased at least one copy of my book (and more). The bookstore owner was extremely happy and we planned the next few events. Then came the holiday shopping season and I got invited to do eight book signings at independent bookstores, from Key Largo to Key West.

Still, doing live events did not help me in getting online reviews from people who weren't my friends. Obviously, I could never mention the word "Amazon" since all independent bookstore owners perceived the company as a new threat to their business interests. Scouring the Internet for more online opportunities I discovered teachers' ezines, which also featured – affordable ads!

For twenty or thirty dollars one could buy a three- or four-line ad in the middle or at the bottom of an ezine. So, I placed an ad and – finally – sold books on Amazon.

Having learned from my friend Rupert how traditional publishers worked I was bowled over at the way Amazon operated. Though, at the time, Amazon's sales portal showed actual sales numbers delayed by one day, I could see sales happening by simply refreshing my Amazon book page every hour.

From that day on, I also used Amazon's sales rank system as a marketing tool. Whenever I contacted the publisher of an online magazine asking if they wanted to review my book I casually mentioned its Amazon sales rank, which almost always led to a positive response.

The reason was easy to figure out: All publishers of online magazines were participants in Amazon's Associate program that allowed them to earn 5–15 percent commission on all sales they generated. Hence, if they reviewed a book that had a good sales rank their odds of making some money were better than if they reviewed an educational toy or other product which wasn't available on Amazon (yet).

Over the next few months, I settled into a routine of seeking book reviews in online and print magazines, giving away free lesson plans to build my mailing list, speaking at school bookfairs and PTA meetings, attending all bookfairs in my region including the Miami Book Fair, sending out my own newsletter, and placing more ads. For a while, my book was even ranked the #1 bestselling alphabet book in its age group on Amazon.

Still, I hadn't given up on getting my book into big bookstores and, at last, I came up with a plan.

The continuing rivalry between the "Earth's Biggest Bookstore (Amazon)" and the "World's Biggest Bookstore (Barnes & Noble)" led to Barnes & Noble's website listing books of which they didn't even have any physical copies, like, for example, my book.

If somebody ordered my book on BarnesandNoble.com, Barnes & Noble couldn't deliver it unless they went through one of the United States' large book distributor companies. So I asked a family friend to buy thirty copies of my book on Barnes & Noble's website and gave him the cash. This move wasn't as crazy as it might look. Obviously, as my book's publisher I'd recover my share of the sale plus I'd also get back the books which I could sell a second time.

The order was "big enough" to get BarnesandNoble.com's attention. Already the next day, a renowned book distributor contacted me and asked if they could sign me on as a vendor so they could order my book. "Could you please return the filled-out paperwork quickly? We would like to expedite the process."

I was ecstatic. Finally, I accomplished what I and thousands of authors had dreamed about – a renowned book distributor came to me asking if they could carry my book. Starting the next day any bookstore in the United States, including all 800+ Barnes & Noble superstores could sell it. As soon as I hung up the phone my husband rushed to buy a bottle of champagne.

Sadly, in the following months, I found out that this move did nothing for me. The book distributor only listed my book in their catalogue but they did not send out an email or a fax introducing my book to bookstores. Instead, it appeared they were waiting for me to promote my book so they could make money distributing it.

Once again, I literally "felt" how Amazon made themselves the darling of all self-publishing authors and small publishers. If I had to do all the work myself, why would I share my earnings with a middleman who did nothing for me, absolutely nothing. In contrast, Amazon was their own distributor and they also gave me tools to market my book.

Like most self-publishing authors, I lived a busy life. I was a mother of two young children who I raised bilingual, a wife who also handled many of her husband's important business matters, and the keeper of our home; which had a very big yard. If I wanted to succeed as a self-publishing author, I needed to work with companies who gave me a fighting chance. Doing everything they did, Amazon put themselves on the top of that list.

- 6 -

A decade later, I sometimes wondered why I, who closely observed Barnes & Noble's power grab of the bookseller industry, didn't see how Amazon was doing the same. I think, first and foremost, it was because Amazon welcomed indie authors with open arms.

This move was so remarkable and radical that I sensed some kind of revolution was about to happen. It was only natural that I wanted to root for the organization that was about to bring change.

The publishing industry's way of doing things had been stagnant for more than 100 years. Literary agents and publishers stressed that it was their job to weed out books that weren't "good enough," which would have been fine if they didn't make mistakes, big mistakes. Like, originally, rejecting Hermann Melville's masterpiece *Moby Dick* with the words, "First we must ask, does it have to be a whale?" Or, telling Louisa May Alcott to "Stick to teaching" when she submitted her manuscript of *Little Women*.

A century later, not much had changed with the exception that editors and publishers started sending form rejection letters so vague that writers could not even know if anybody actually read their submissions. My own work had never been rejected but I had learned a thing or two about the process.

A year before self-publishing my alphabet book, I submitted a manuscript of a math book to a big publisher. Much to my surprise, already six weeks later, an editor contacted me to let me know that he thought my manuscript was "quite promising."

However, instead of things moving forward, I got strung along for six months until I learned that the editor "abruptly left the company." And, when I tried to find out what the editor's replacement thought about my submission, he told me that somebody discarded all of his predecessor's files because the company was "going in a new direction."

This experience and other stories I heard led me to believe that if writers found an easier way to publish books, most of them would take that other option in a heartbeat.

Similarly, in 1998, when I self-published my alphabet book, big bookstores had no plans to host book signings of self-published authors, regardless of how much press coverage the books had received. This was even more astonishing when one considered that the opportunity to do live events was the one thing where big bookstores had the edge. Their biggest competitor, Amazon, could not host live events.

To me it looked as if, stoked by reports that Amazon was in the red, most industry insiders thought (or hoped) that Amazon would fail, hence there was no reason to change their ways of doing things.

Meanwhile, Jeff Bezos gave people who loved books but whose needs were not addressed by the traditional systems the tools to create their own space.

Today, the concept of "winning customers' trust" by giving them a free product or a starter program is touted by most marketing experts. Still, I have yet to see somebody who is more generous than Jeff Bezos was at the time.

He gave all authors a recognized venue to sell their books, a space to garner book reviews, and the option to brag about their book's sales rank – for free.

In the nineties, these offerings were nothing short of miraculous. At the time, authors had to get on the bestseller list of *The New York Times*, *Publishers Weekly*, *The Wall Street Journal* or *USA Today*, to gain these kinds of PR tools.

With his Associate Program, Bezos also gave people who didn't want to write a book but had a mailing list of people who might want to buy books the opportunity to make some money on the side. This group included teachers who needed additional income to buy supplies for their classrooms, people who hated their jobs and would have rather run a bookstore, and people who had websites that promoted a specific topic or a hobby. Because Amazon's marketing tools were perfectly tailored to these people's needs, they rushed to direct their friends and acquaintances to Amazon.

- 7 -

Still, while I didn't see, or didn't want to see, that Jeff Bezos was preparing for a power grab of multiple industries, I did notice things other people never saw:

From the beginning, I believed that Jeff Bezos likes to speak in double meanings.

When he talked about Amazon's mission to be the world's most customer-obsessed company he didn't only talk about Amazon's buyers – the readers. To Jeff Bezos, indie authors, small publishers, and Amazon affiliates were customers too. He wanted to meet and even exceed their ambitions, too.

It was this concept that convinced me that Jeff Bezos was a business genius.

Whereas the traditional players in the book selling industry only tried to hone down on the needs of their existing customers ("Would you also like to sip coffee while you browse our magazines for free?"), Amazon asked completely new questions, like "What do marginalized booklovers want?" Most importantly, "What do writers, teachers, hobbyists, and buyers of specialty books want?"

I also believed that, from the beginning, Jeff Bezos avoided even hinting at the entire scope of his business plan. Though in his first interviews he always stressed that he decided to sell books because there are more items in this shopping category than in others, this fact could not be the sole reason why he wanted to sell books. Because it made no sense.

Considering that the Internet was relatively new it would take years until a majority of book buyers would buy online. Meanwhile, Bezos would have to cover high costs for personnel traditional bookstores did not employ, like workers who packed and shipped books and computer whizzes who handled everything from upkeeping the webstore to making sure that online payments were secure.

Most importantly, by selling only books Amazon didn't offer anything that could not be done by just about any big bookstore. I knew that for a fact. During my student years in Vienna, Austria, I wanted to buy a book about the history of special effects which had been published in the United States. It was easy. I just walked into a Viennese bookstore, gave the owner the ISBN-number and ordered the book. It arrived seven weeks later.

If I combined this knowledge with the fact that Jeff Bezos was courting indie authors like the fairy godmother herself, I could not help but think that beyond selling books Jeff Bezos also planned to revolutionize the entire publishing industry, which, inevitably, would be a homerun because most writers were unhappy with how the traditional world of publishing and bookselling worked.

Years later, I felt that my theory was proven right when, in 2011, I read in *WIRED magazine* that Jeff Bezos introduced the Kindle Fire to renowned tech writer Steven Levy by saying that the Kindle Fire was a culmination of what he'd been doing for fifteen years. 2011 minus 15 equals 1996. Therefore, it appeared that, from the get-go, Jeff Bezos planned to create a publishing platform. Maybe, Bezos' wife MacKenzie, who studied under renowned writer Toni Morrison told her husband about the plights of authors and that writers would go the extra mile for the first person who'd help them publish their manuscripts.

- 8 -

By the year 2000, my publishing endeavors had turned into a nice and very satisfying side-hustle. I was even thinking that maybe I could publish my math book sometime soon. But later that year my husband died, unexpectedly. And, in an instant, everything I had been doing became irrelevant.

Suddenly, there weren't enough hours in the day to do everything I needed to do – being the best parent I could be, teaching at the local high school, writing lesson plans, running the household, making sure that the weeds didn't overtake the yard, and taking my kids to their swim training. Because my husband and I immigrated to the United States I had little help. At least, I felt I could not impose on my friends all the time.

Naturally, I could have gone back to Austria where all my and Florian's family lived. But, after pondering the issue for a while I decided that I did not want my children who just lost their father to also lose the only home they ever knew, their friends, and their school. They needed as much stability as I could provide. Taking them to a country where everybody spoke German and enrolling them in a completely different school system would probably destabilize their lives even more.

Two years later it became obvious that I was making things too hard for myself. Life in the Florida Keys was too expensive; everything was priced for tourists, not for widowed moms. So I moved my family to Wilmington, North Carolina.

Thinking that I'd find a job relatively quickly, I decided to buy a few stocks, more specifically – Amazon stocks.

"Don't do it, Amazon is a fad," the broker warned. "Buy oil instead. ExxonMobile will do well for you."

"I am an environmentalist," I snarled, "I don't buy Big Oil." Then, I purchased thirty Amazon stocks for fifty dollars each.

Unfortunately, neither one of my assumptions worked out. I could not find a full-time job but had to accept a part-time position and Amazon's stock kept dropping. The latter was made worse by the fact that the stock market seemed to prove the broker right. Was I some kind of fool who believed in a company nobody else seemed to take seriously? Two years later I sold my Amazon stocks, at a loss of $20 each.

Though, in the years to come, most people would have remembered this decision with regret, in a kind of "I could have been a contender"-way, in the bigger scope of things it did not matter to me.

A few months after I bought these stocks my kid brother Michael died and the year after my best friend since teenage days. Losing three persons dearest to my heart within five years taught me what all the money in the world cannot buy.

Finally, in January 2006, Lady Fortuna smiled upon me, for a split second. I did not recognize the moment as such, but I still took her offer.

I was at FedexKinkos, faxing my resume to a few potential employers when the store manager chatted me up. Noticing what I was doing, she asked me what kind of job I was looking for. And, after a brief conversation she offered me the position of Fedex shipping specialist. Though I didn't really want to work in the retail industry, in a way, the offer was appealing. My daughter needed braces. Though my part-time job was better paid than Fedex's it did not come with health insurance. And so, I accepted the worst paid job of my career.

Most astoundingly, this $9.67 per hour job turned out to be the most important job I ever held. Two years later, this employment would help me land and keep a job while millions of Americans were unemployed, during the Great Recession. But, in 2006, I did not know that; I was just trying to learn from the industry leader in transportation.

Another reason for accepting the job was that I was fascinated with Fedex's logistics operations for many years. In 1982 or '83 when I was still working in Austria's movie industry, my boss asked me to represent the company at the documentary film festival in Seefeld/Austria while he attended the Cannes Film Festival in France which took place the same week.

It was a huge honor for me; certainly, I was going to prove myself worthy of his trust. While other attendees went to check out the "crown jewel" of alpine golf courses, the Seefeld-Wildmoos golf course, and hung out at the Casino Seefeld, I did what my boss expected me to do and watched all showings of all documentaries, 9-to-5, on all three days. That's how I learned about Fedex's operations even before they began serving Europe.

Fedex's festival entry was a documentary that explained how the company handled their 1-day deliveries, by transporting all packages to Memphis, Tennessee and redistributing them from there. It was awe inspiring. If truth be told, two or three years later, I could not even remember the two films my company entered in the festival, but I never forgot Fedex's documentary.

For this reason, I was very interested in learning more about the company's inner workings.

As commonly known, Fedex uses best practices to ensure that all its shipments reach their destinations on time and in perfect condition. There was only one way – the best way – to ship customers' documents and goods. Eager to learn, I watched educational videos about the different types of cardboard boxes, packing fragile goods, building custom-made boxes, taping boxes so they would not break open on rattling conveyors, and much more. After four weeks of practicing, I could build a perfect custom-made box in under ten minutes.

Three months later, when Fedex decided to create the new position of Fedex subject matter expert at all FedexKinkos stores, my store manager overlooked the assistant manager and appointed me as the best suited employee.

The position came with amazing educational perks. Not only did I have access to all of Fedex's online courses, including from at home, twice per month I participated in the subject matter experts' phone conference where I learned specialized knowledge from processing haz-mat shipments to creating all required documentation for overseas shipments. Best of all, I even got the opportunity to take six-sigma courses related to transportation – for free.

Still, when, a year later, I got the opportunity to start working for a well-established construction company, I had to leave Fedex. Working as preconstruction services coordinator, I'd be earning a much better income.

- 9 -

Nine months later, in November 2007, Amazon made headline news when the company released a revolutionary gizmo – an ebook reader named Kindle. When I heard this news, I almost fainted.

I always knew it! I guessed it!

Clearly, Jeff Bezos realized that the hundreds of thousands of writers who wanted to publish their books were an untapped market.

The personal computer revolution helped aspiring writers immensely. Starting in the mid-nineties, organizing research files, fixing typos, and editing drafts became easier, hence writers could concentrate on the real task – creative writing. At the same time the publishing industry missed the digital revolution in an almost Kodakesque way. They started sending vague form rejection letters which suggested to writers that nobody actually read their submissions. Last but not least, in authors' forums on the Internet, handed-down stories of what some authors did with their rejection letters began having an effect on writers who felt ignored.

All in all, it was one of these moments in history when a group of people who felt marginalized were ready to follow any "savior," in this case, the first company that would help them publish their works.

Even better for Amazon – disappointed writers as well as self-published writers were a group of people willing to give 110 percent, every day. I knew this for a fact because I met them. Before and after I published my alphabet book, I went to more than a dozen bookfairs, as a visitor and a self-published author.

At the Miami Book Fair 1997, I attended the presentation of a self-published author who talked about how he managed to self-publish his first novel without having to put a second mortgage on his house. His book was an impressive looking 400-page hardcover book – with dust jacket. The author talked for an hour and took questions for another two. His presentation drew the most visitors at any of the outdoor booths I saw in downtown Miami.

The writer had a corner booth which allowed visitors to approach his venue from two sides. Still, there was not enough room for the more than 100 people who wanted to hear his story. We ended up standing shoulder-to-shoulder, sweating in 85 degrees heat. But, nobody left and everybody had at least one question.

In South Florida, most book fairs were hot outdoor events. Still, I never saw a self-published author lounging in a chair and watching visitors pass by at any of the bookfairs I visited. Self-published authors never stopped promoting their books, because, to them, their books were their babies.

For these reasons I believed that the invention of the Kindle announced the dawn of a new era, similar to when Gutenberg invented the printing press. Just like Gutenberg's invention undid the power the church and the nobility exerted as they decided which books should be hand-copied by monks, Amazon's invention would undo the power literary agents and publishers exercised over the book industry.

In my opinion, Jeff Bezos was a new Gutenberg. Even better, he was also a defender of the First Amendment. Starting now, people who had something to say would no longer be limited to printing flyers, like the hundreds of thousands of flyers I saw getting printed at FedexKinkos.

- 10 -

Unfortunately, while I was dying to see how the Kindle worked, I could not afford buying one. Priced at $399 the Kindle was too expensive for a single mother of two high schoolers. Especially, since something seemed to be wrong with the economy.

By February 2008, the danger became all too clear. Since I also served as the assistant to the Vice President of Preconstruction, I found out that none of the owners whose contracts we won in the preceding few weeks got financing from their banks. It scared the wits out of me. I knew that if banks did not lend money it meant that the United States was heading for a recession. When, three months later, I was laid off with one month of severance pay, I started searching for a new job the next morning.

Though I applied for every job under the sun, I received only one invitation to interview – from a non-vessel operating common carrier (NVOCC) and freight forwarder. The pressure to ace the interview was immense because I had never shipped a container. Still, courtesy of Fedex's excellent educational program, I looked knowledgeable and got the job.

A few weeks later things got worse. Month after month, hundreds of thousands of Americans got laid off. Things felt so bad that I did not enter the house when I came home; I did not want to bring the stress inside. Instead, I sat under the big tree in my backyard, where I often cried from exhaustion, hoping that my children would not see me.

But – I made it. While the Great Recession raged on, I shipped hundreds of containers loaded with expensive goods of all sorts to the Middle East. Furniture, frozen orange juice, pizza dough, car parts, electric panels, water heaters, all kinds of machinery, roofing paper, and even hand sanitizer – I shipped it all.

When in Spring 2010, my son graduated high school, I cried again, during the ceremony. This time, it was tears of happiness. I fulfilled the promise I made to myself that I would make sure that my children got the opportunities they deserved. It'd be another year until my daughter would graduate but having come that far I knew I'd make it.

By the time my daughter graduated, I was already promoted to 'sales & marketing' at the NVOCC and freight forwarder. I felt it was an improbable success. At a time when many people were just getting back to work I was getting promoted. Thrilled with the way things went, I tried to analyze which of my action steps helped to make it happen. I believed it was because – instead of following somebody else's plan I took "my life's building blocks" and rearranged them to build "a different staircase."

Eventually, I came up with the plan to write a book about what I learned – an inspirational life-skills book with 41 stories everybody could relate to. Of course, I was going to publish it on Amazon.

- 11 -

I released *Naked Determination: 41 Stories About Overcoming Fear* in 2012. The book offered a new approach to an over-produced product – the self-help book.

Being fifty years old, I believed that all but a few self-help books were hopelessly outdated. These days, one could find the answers they presented on the Internet. Besides that, most of us did not even need the advice. In real life, most of us always knew what we were supposed to do. If we did not do it, it was because we were afraid. Afraid that others would laugh about us, that doing what we had to do was too hard, or that we would fail. (The idea that somebody would abstain from doing something they knew they should do because they were greedy did not occur to me.)

I believed the best way to get on the road to success was to find inspiration in our past, in our own stories. After all, even if we lost everything, we still owned our stories.

And so, I wrote an entertaining book full of wild-but-true personal anecdotes that showed how all of us can use our personal history to overcome the fear that comes with trying to move on to bigger things.

Designing my first ebook I figured out another huge advantage of ebook publishing – I could add pictures that helped to tell my stories and "sprinkle" them throughout the text where they belonged – in color!

I was in love with ebook publishing, the Kindle, and the second Printing Revolution.

In 2014, I finished writing *Naked Words: The Effective 157-Word Email*, picked a cool launch date – Pi-Day 3/14/15 – and offered the book for review to the *Success* magazine. They accepted it! Seeing my book featured in the magazine's print edition August 2015 was beyond thrilling.

Next, I wrote *Naked Truths About Getting Book Reviews on Amazon* (by top reviewer Gisela Hausmann).

At the time, helping fledgling self-published authors learn how they could get their books noticed seemed like a great idea. Many of Amazon's earliest self-published authors released really neat works. Since they wrote their manuscripts at a time when they believed they had to convince a publisher to accept their work, these writers honed their craft, took writers' classes, and burned the midnight oil trying to create a book that would withstand the critical scrutiny of literary agents and publishers.

However, as time passed, things changed. All kinds of "entrepreneurs" tried to use Amazon's offerings, including people whose main business seemed to be talking other people into writing books. Since many of them tried to attract people who never even wrote a blog, they wanted to sell programs that would teach the newcomers what to write and how to write.

Some "book marketers" began holding online seminars about "Learn how to write books as a means of building a passive income." Many of them made it a habit to mention bestsellers such as *Harry Potter* and *Fifty Shades of Grey,* as if it was easy to write a bestseller.

Over time, these marketers' efforts to ride in Amazon's wake created problems.

Many writers who discovered their love for writing only because they wanted to "build a passive income" resorted to cheating when they found out that their books did not sell automatically.

They formed "street teams" which was a cool name for hordes of writers who followed each other and worked on making each others' books look good, as a team effort. They also awarded each others' books with 5-star reviews and became members of authors' clubs in which everybody had to buy other authors' books and read and review them to drive up each others' sales ranks.

While there was nothing wrong with these efforts per se, obviously, Amazon had to take a stand against these activities once it was clear that they were "organized efforts."

Again other "entrepreneurs" copied Amazon's list of top reviewers and gave it as a gift or as a bonus to people who followed their programs, which led to Amazon's top reviewers' Inboxes getting filled with thousands of ludicrous emails.

Such as, "... I wrote a nonfiction book and since this is the first book I am trying to sell on Amazon I am not sure what the protocol is. My book is about how to write any book, without any prior education in writing. Would you be interested in reviewing it? ..."

Probably worst of all, on Fiverr, hundreds of contractors advertised, "Will write and post reviews... from multiple accounts..." Apparently, they did not know that posting fake reviews is a violation of the Federal Trade Commission's truth-in-advertising laws.

In short, it was the Wild West days of online reviews.

- 12 -

As it could be expected Amazon hit back and tightened their algorithms, so they'd find the cheaters (or most of them) and kick them out. They also sued the Fiverr contractors who offered to write fake reviews. Still, hundreds of thousands of honest authors and Amazon vendors suffered.

It was hard to compete against others who purchased fake reviews or ran other schemes. Especially little indie authors' efforts to market their books fair and square always fell short. Since Amazon presented ads in between the books' main representation and the books' reviews, customers had to scroll over that ad section where they got to see other books (or products), some of which featured hundreds of reviews that were acquired "almost overnight."

Most baffling to me was that – apparently – Amazon did not have a forward-looking action plan or a task force whose mission was to hinder fraud *before* it happened. Many author blogs told stories of how indie authors had to make Amazon aware of phony schemes which were happening on their ecommerce platform. The way it looked, Amazon only reacted to fraud.

Because Amazon changed their reviewer guidelines, I was forced to update my book *Naked Truth* not even a year after I published it. Since I had to dive into the subject matter again, I also wrote a second book for Amazon's product vendors and also translated it into German. The latter two received quite a bit of media coverage, including on *Bloomberg* and in Austrian business publications. I was happy. There still were opportunities.

A few months later, I had an irritating experience, at a Halloween party, of all places.

"Gisela, meet John Doe," the hostess said. "He just moved to town and is still looking for his dream job." John and I nodded at each other.

"Welcome to Greenville," I said. "I bet you'll love it here. Even though it is a smaller city, Greenville has International flair. I used to live on the coast, for more than twenty years. But, I got tired of evacuating from hurricanes. So, now I live 'in the woods'." I laughed politely.

"Ha," John smiled. "I lived on the coast too. In Charleston. But I was ready for a change. So, I finally quit my job and moved to the other end of the state. I didn't need that sh*t. Pardon my language."

"Please," I said, "no need to apologize, all of us have felt that way. Who'd you work for?"

"Createspace," he replied dryly.

I almost spilled my drink. "CREATESPACE? You mean Amazon's paperback printing division?"

John looked at me, surprised. "You know them?"

"Well, yes," I replied cautiously. "I am the author of a few books. Since they were printed in Charleston, you might have been involved in their production." I tried a compliment. "Great quality, the books. Not one problem. Never, ever."

"Yep," he said, "but like I said, I am done with them." Then, he excused himself.

When twenty minutes later I went to get a new drink, he was gone. Which was odd.

Days later, I still pondered how I should understand this man's reaction. Clearly, he did not like working for Createspace. But – Why? Maybe, living up to Createspace's/Amazon's quality standards had been too much for him? Or maybe, he hated working long hours?

Surely, it had to be one of these options. But why did he leave so shortly after the event started?

- 13 -

Over the next two years I wrote more books and updated others but, in general, publishing and marketing books on Amazon's platform became more difficult.

Fake reviews were only the beginning. Eventually, writers (not authors) rephrased or even stole entire works from other authors and tried to sell them on Amazon. There were also writers (not authors) who created multiple copies of the same book with different titles and/or covers. Other writers (not authors) tried to scam Amazon's KDP program.

Though Amazon fought every problem, on their platform as well in courts of law, the problems never seemed to end. Aside from getting featured in hundreds of authors' blogs, the scams also made headline news in major publications.

*

September 27, 2016

Revealed: How one Amazon Kindle scam made millions of dollars" (*ZDNet Zero Day*/ Zack Whittaker)

*

September 7, 2017

Amazon targets abuse of Kindle e-book platform to increase reviews, royalties (*Seattle Times*/Matt Day)

*

Oct. 12, 2017

"From Amazon, a Change That Hurts Authors" (*New York Times*/Douglas Preston)

*

September 20, 2017

"Amazon has laid out exactly how to game its self-publishing platform" (*Quartz*/Thu-Huong Ha)

*

April 7, 2018

"Amazon Won Arbitration That Addresses The Six-Figure 'Book Stuffing' Kindle Scam" (*Forbes*/Adam Rowe)

*

June 13, 2018

"Kindle Unlimited Book Stuffing Scam Earns Millions and Amazon Isn't Stopping It" (*Inc.com*/ Minda Zetlin)

*

August 10, 2018

"Amazon self-published authors: Our books were banned for no reason" (*Yahoo*/JP Mangalindan)

*

March 28, 2019
"Plagiarism, 'book-stuffing', clickfarms ... the rotten side of self-publishing" (*The Guardian*/Alison Flood)

*

By May 2019, I felt I needed to take a hard look at what happened to my writing and publishing ambitions. Clearly, Amazon's publishing platform was no longer what it used to be. The second printing-press revolution happened, but in addition to giving all authors the freedom to publish their books it also attracted all kinds of shady characters.

Personally, I did not think that the cheaters and scammers were out to hurt indie authors. Even most thieves would not steal coins out of a beggar's hat. I believed that it was headlines such as "Jeff Bezos Boosts Fortune by $12 Billion in a Day on Amazon Surge" on April 26, 2018 (*Bloomberg*/ Tom Metcalf and Jack Witzig) which caused a certain kind of people to think, "Well, he won't miss a couple of grand." Most likely, the crooks never understood that they weren't hurting Jeff Bezos, but indie authors and other Amazon vendors, financially. Therefore, the cheating and scamming would probably never end.

With all that in mind, I decided to take a break from writing and publishing.

- 14 -

In the summer of 2019, I found myself in limbo. I left a long-term employment believing that I accepted a cool job offer from a company where I'd be able to utilize my German language skills. Alas, within three weeks it became clear that this company had sold themselves as something different than they really were. We split amicably and I was reading job ads again.

After four weeks of searching two potential employers emerged; one was a construction company who was looking to fill a marketing position and the other a bank who wanted to hire a communications trainer. I passed two interviews with one company and three with the other but wasn't really thrilled about either one of the two opportunities.

For the second time in this century I worried that the United States could be sliding into a recession, maybe already after the Christmas holidays. Though President Trump kept touting his great successes I believed that the economy was hyped and so was the stock market. After New Year, stock owners might interpret any kind of pullback as a sign to cash out their gains, which could lead to a recession in the next two quarters. In this scenario, both of the jobs I interviewed for might turn out to be risky choices. Typically, in a recession, the construction industry is the first to run into problems and, since banks always watch their expenses, they too would probably cut nonessential positions. If only I could find a cool job with a cool company which was recession-proof.

Unsure if I should ignore my uneasiness, I examined the very latest job ads – again.

The local Amazon delivery station was looking for associates.

I pondered the idea. Years ago, I applied at Amazon a few times, but only for positions related to the book industry. At the time, Amazon did not have a logistics division. If I grabbed this job, I could probably work up my way relatively quickly. After all, I had six years of experience in logistics.

Also – Hadn't I just read that Amazon wanted to buy shipping containers? If I excelled at working in this environment, maybe I could transfer to their ocean freight department? Come to think of it, working at this warehouse would be perfect. Though I had years of experience in the transportation industry, I had little experience with anything related to warehousing.

I called my best friend who worked in the transportation industry all her life.

"What do you think about working at Amazon?"

"Well, why not? What'd you be doing there?"

"I don't know. It's a warehouse job related to last-mile deliveries, but that's what's interesting. I have not done more than half-a-dozen warehouse consolidations. That's probably not good enough for Amazon. Everything their logistics division does is related to warehousing. Plus, if I am right with my suspicion that a recession is coming..."

My friend burst out in laughter; in the recent past, we had discussed my concern more than once. "You and your suspicions. But, no, Amazon would not be affected by a recession. That's for sure."

"Exactly. Also, I really love the company."

"Try it."

I applied, was asked to do a drug test and got hired. When the Human Resources person asked which shift I wanted to work, I chose the night shift. While most people hate working the graveyard shift, I welcomed the opportunity. For years, working Monday through Friday 8-to-5 forced me to sacrifice precious vacation days whenever I needed to visit a doctor, run an errand, or worked on a home improvement project. I planned to update my kitchen and my bathroom before the kids visited for Christmas. Painting walls would be much easier during daylight hours.

- 15 -

On my first day of work I was welcomed by an Amazon learning ambassador who conducted the training for me and the three other newbies. His presentation about the actual work was pretty basic. This surprised me. Since it's widely known that working at Amazon is all about hitting performance goals, I was sure that we'd be drilled in best practices. However, the word did not even come up. Finally, the instructor said something that startled me, "If a package drops, don't make any weird moves to catch it. We can replace everything, but we cannot replace you."

The comment stunned me because I had never considered this angle. Indeed, Amazon wasn't a shipper like Fedex, UPS, or the United States Postal Service; Amazon was supplier and shipper rolled into one. Therefore, they'd be able to replace damaged items without any fuss. But, that's not how the transportation industry works.

Typically, transportation companies try to define themselves by using the sentence, "We treat your shipment with utmost care." It's a pivotal declaration because if a problem arises these words will be held against the shipper. I knew that Fedex trained their employees to handle packages with utmost care and that their customers had come to expect this service. If a doorbell camera caught a Fedex driver dropping a package, the footage often ended up on the local news and Fedex rushed to assure their customers that this was an isolated incident. Yet, at Amazon, the entire topic wasn't even a consideration.

Obviously, this aspect of their logistics operations helped Amazon meet their tight timelines and, at the same time, it disadvantaged all other shipping carriers who transported Amazon's merchandise. Fedex, UPS and the United States Postal Service had to take their time to treat packages more carefully because they had no option to replace damaged or lost goods.

The operations at my new workplace, DSC3, were easy to understand. Throughout the night thousands of packages and envelopes arrived from various fulfillment centers in the region.

Once at DSC3, all items had to be inducted so Amazon's computer system recorded that they had arrived. At our facility, inbound items weren't inducted by machines, instead, people, "inductors," scanned them with big handheld scanners. The scanners also spit out the labels that listed the number of the bag into which each package had to be placed.

After getting inducted and having a label affixed, the packages got transported to the stowing area on one of three conveyors. There, "pickers" took the items off the conveyors and placed them on their designated bakers' racks alongside the conveyors.

Behind each of the bakers' racks was an aisle lined with shelves perpendicular to the bakers' racks. The "stowers" worked in these aisles; they stowed the boxes and envelopes into their designated bags.

All bags had to be fully stowed by 6:00 a.m. the next morning when Amazon's delivery drivers arrived to pick them up and deliver the goods.

Overall, the huge warehouse was as clean as a 5-star hotel. Along all walls and in every corner stood water coolers and vending machines that dispensed safety vests, gloves, and other equipment. Though I read dozens of articles about the abuse of workers at Amazon facilities the people I saw were chatting and laughing while working, and all of them seemed quite happy or at least content.

The crowning jewel of the facility was its lunchroom which was the opposite of all lunchrooms at big corporations I ever set foot in. Whereas typical lunchrooms were dingy places, unworthy of any Fortune 500 company, Amazon's breakroom radiated, "This is a place where you can relax and recharge." I saw a pinball machine, a Pac-Man arcade machine, two basketball hoops, two TV-monitors and a comfortable looking sofa, as well as four vending machines, including one with all healthy choices and another one that offered hot beverages free of charge. Naturally, there were also refrigerators, microwave ovens, more coffee machines, and the usual stuff.

Still, there was one feature I appreciated even more than all the others – the lunchroom's colorful walls. In fact, I had been waiting to see walls like this my entire professional life.

To me, the design of a lunchroom is an indicator of how a company sees their employees – as valuable assets or expendables. Since colored paint costs the same as white paint, why would any company designer choose the most boring color? Unless the employer didn't care.

In contrast, DSC3's lunchroom had vibrant Amazon-orange walls with a big Prime-blue border which featured Amazon's leadership principles: "Think Big", "Invent and simplify", "Have backbone; disagree and commit", and, of course, "We're not competitor obsessed, we're customer obsessed."

To me, it was perfection. Clearly, Amazon went beyond trying to create a positive atmosphere, they also used their walls to share their brand message. I was in awe and could see myself working at a place with that spirit.

- 16 -

After the brief introduction about working at DSC3 and touring the facility, it was time to practice "picking packages."

The task sounded simple enough: "Watch the conveyor and look for packages and envelopes whose sticker lists a number from your section of baker's racks. Grab the items and put each on the baker's rack with the corresponding number. The stowers will take 'em from the other side and stow 'em away."

However, in practice, the task had its challenges. Whereas most videos of Amazon warehouses I ever saw showed only conveyors on which all items were spaced out neatly, apparently, at smaller delivery stations like DSC3 things were different. Since the inductors worked independently, quite often, bunches of items ended up in crowded piles on the conveyors.

This made it impossible for the pickers to spot all items that belonged into their section of bakers' racks. As a result, the pickers had to run up and down along the conveyor to hand-deliver some of the packages where they belonged. One quick look at the floor told me that if I'd get assigned to do this job, I'd have to buy shoes with air soles; the warehouse had a concrete floor.

On the other hand, "stowing" looked like fun. It reminded me of playing the video game Tetris quite obsessively, in the late eighties. That game was all about quickly filling spaces with different shaped blocks without leaving any gaps. Like in a real-life, 3-D version of Tetris the stowers took the items from the bakers' rack and stowed them into the bags as quickly as possible. Since there were four rows of bags on each side, the stowers had to "play multiple games," simultaneously.

Stowing was considered the most challenging task at DSC3. To hit the target rate of stowing 300+ items per hour (one item every 12 seconds) the stowers needed to make on-the-fly decisions about where to place boxes and envelopes without knowing the sizes and shapes of the items that needed to be stowed into the same bag later.

Laying boxes flat into a bag was a no-no, because if a larger package was placed on top of a smaller package the empty space below the larger package never got filled. Therefore, all boxes had to be stowed standing on their long side or short side.

Laying envelopes which everybody at the warehouse called jiffies flat into a bag was a no-no too. Since many of the jiffies contained bottles and other, bigger items, any box that was placed on top of them could slide out of the bags. Ideally, all jiffies were supposed to go on top of the boxes.

After observing the pickers and the stowers for a few minutes I made my decision. Since I was a person who liked to set her own pace, I would aim to become a stower. To me, it seemed easier trying to find my own rhythm than keeping up with the pace of the conveyor.

After lunch, I got my first chance to try out my stowing skills. Standing in an aisle and inspecting bags somebody else had started I thought I could have done a better job but there was no time to evaluate things further. The picker on the other side of the baker's rack at the end of the aisle kept piling up packages that needed to be stowed. Only when twenty minutes later I felt I had things under control, I rearranged a few packages to achieve a better space distribution inside some of the bags. As I stepped back to check my work, the picker stuck her head through the now empty baker's rack.

"Hey there, if you are done here you better knock down the packages in the next aisle."

"Hello too," I said. And then, "No, they told me that this is my aisle. I am supposed to work here."

The woman on the other side of the baker's rack looked slightly annoyed. "Yup, but when you are done, you needa help somewhere else. I have no room to put packages in 23-24. Can you go over there, n-o-w?"

I was irritated. Why hadn't anybody told me? The learning ambassador hadn't said a beep about other aisles. I rushed to 23-24 to take care of a wall of packages that would have impressed any person who likes big walls. Eventually, I came to find out that at my delivery station, but probably at other warehouses too, Amazon relied on peer education, which isn't necessarily a hallmark of best practices.

- 17 -

In general, all work at the warehouse was extremely physical. At DSC3's dock, associates unloaded trailers which amounted to moving pallets, unloading boxes and envelopes, and lifting packages of all sizes for six hours. Other employees inducted the items which was easy work but holding the big and heavy scanner was not. Again others worked at various positions along the conveyors, diverting and picking off packages.

The only employees whose pace of work was not dictated by the speed of the conveyor were the stowers. Whereas everybody who worked along the conveyor had to deal with whatever the conveyor brought along more or less immediately (including lifting boxes up to fifty pounds), the stowers could decide in which order they wanted to stow the items.

Probably because stowing offered the most freedom, the stowers' performance rates were looked at constantly. They were also published on "the list" from best to worst, every day.

This list helped Amazon to enforce their expectations. Stowers who did not hit the target rate used it to track their progress. Naturally, "the list" also encouraged competition. When I myself tried to beat our two best stowers, I even went so far as to enlist the help of some pickers. Three girls helped me a lot. Whenever they had a short break, they sorted all packages on the bakers' rack by their respective bag numbers so I could stow faster. But, even stowing at a rate of more than 1,000 items during the first two hours (one item every 7.2 seconds) I could never beat these two guys.

On the negative side, "the list" probably chased away people who could not or did not want to put up with Amazon's performance-driven work culture. Frequently, I noticed that a stower who complained about how difficult it was to hit the rate just did not show up anymore.

Still, though everybody worked hard most employees at DSC3 seemed happy, including me. There was probably a simple explanation for that. Working at the delivery station was the equivalent of doing an intense workout. Since good workouts promote the release of endorphins, also referred to as "feel-good" chemicals, especially during the first two of the three work sessions most employees felt good.

Over the next few weeks, I reached the goal of stowing 300+ packages per hour for six hours, lost six pounds, made friends, and kept working on my plan to show my managers that I was capable of doing greater things.

Then, one late-night break, one of my friends asked me, "So, what are you doing here, at a delivery station? You don't look as if you do warehouse work."

I laughed and said, "Well, I am here to learn. I have worked in logistics for almost six years. Shipping forty-foot-high cube ocean containers, twenty-foot containers, reefers, LCLs, hazmat shipments, inland trucking, airfreight, Fedex – I have done it all. But I have barely any experience with warehousing. So, I thought, instead of applying at Amazon Logistics who'd probably ignore me because I have no experience in warehousing, why not work here for a while and then try climbing through the ranks."

My friend's eyebrows formed a V. Then, the friend said, "Well, here you are going to have to kiss a lot of a** to climb anywhere. Trust me."

I almost choked on my coffee. "Come again?"

"Well, what do you think how anybody gets promoted here? Haven't you noticed that some of the people who are in charge behave as if they were still in high school? I mean the whole game of liking and not liking people? And, if you dare to make a suggestion they don't like, you immediately get punished and they'll assign you to a position you don't wanna do."

I giggled. "Yes, I noticed that. Twice I found myself picking packages which I hate. Still, I thought embodying Amazon's leadership principles "Invent and simplify" and "Insist on the Highest Standards" would help me move up the ranks."

"You can forget that. Nobody cares. Nobody. Trust me."

- 18 -

Later that night, on my way home, I thought of the printer who used to work at Createspace. Was this what he meant when he summed up his job with the explicit word he used?

Also, it was impossible to deny that my friend at DSC3 had a point. Just the other day, one of the assistant shift managers who seemed not to like me visited me in my aisle and demanded to know why my stowing rate had dropped. And, when I told her that I had to rearrange a few packages in a few of the bags so I could put more items into them she yelled at me that I should just close the bags that were too messy and open new bags.

Though I was appalled at how she talked to me I also noticed some desperation in her voice. Were our stowing rates a criterion of her job performance evaluation? And, if that was the case why didn't the managers deal with the real problem – that some of the temporary workers who got hired for "(Holiday) Peak 2019" did not follow the guidelines for stowing? But while I worried that Christmas gifts might get damaged the assistant shift manager only seemed to care about the numbers on her laptop screen.

Come to think about it, I had many questions. But not all problems started at DSC3.

For my standards, way too many of the thousands of packages that arrived every day were already dented, torn, or even crushed to the point that they looked like accordions before our team even unloaded them. Placing these items on a roller conveyor could only make things worse.

Why wasn't it Amazon's policy that the associates who loaded the items at the fulfillment centers sorted out the damaged boxes and fulfilled these orders anew? Didn't Jeff Bezos worry about what Amazon's customers would think?

Over the entrance door of DSC3's warehouse hung a sign which said to "always start with the customer" and "work backwards." But, having worked for many companies on two continents, I had never seen an organization that seemed to care less about "the customers" than Amazon Logistics. Sure – Amazon was going to deliver in two days. But what good did that do if the goods arrived damaged?

Just a short while ago, I stowed a toy, some kind of horse or unicorn with a rainbow-colored mane which wasn't packaged in a cardboard box but in its original, pink box with window. Seeing the cute thing reminded me of buying toys for my own daughter, more specifically – toys that were supposed to bring "magic" into her life, after her father died.

Because the pink box was unsuitable for transport, one third of it had been crushed. The way it looked the damage had been caused by the machine which applied the address labels to the boxes at the fulfillment center. Why did they send us this package? We only reordered broken items. But, while the "horsie" appeared to be undamaged the whole thing did not look like a pretty gift.

Of course, we at DSC3 broke items too; usually, on the conveyor. Then again, why did the fulfillment centers package bottles which contained liquids into plastic bags? Wasn't it obvious that the one or other would break? Didn't Amazon have data that told them which items were prone to break open on conveyors?

Typically, we found out about such incidents when one of us noticed that a package or an envelope leaked liquid. Though upon discovering a leaking item, every time, hell broke loose, it was never about the damage but only about the concern that the package or envelope might contain a liquid which was classified as hazardous material.

Associates who touched a leaking item were required to immediately stop working, and wash and sanitize their hands (even if the liquid smelled like facial toner). Next, the clean-up team got called and finally, without much fuss, the broken item was reordered. But – Who paid for the loss? Amazon or the vendor?

Another source of irritation were Amazon's white-blue lightweight plastic mailers. Because they are rather slippery they slid off other items and other items slid off them. Even worse, since they were too big for many of the light items they contained, every night, the huge fans at the warehouse blew some of the mailers out of the bags.

Whenever, upon coming back from the break at 2:45 a.m., I found white-blue mailers on the floor I could not help but wonder if Amazon's designers had tested the mailers for usage "in the field" – at a warehouse – or only in a lab. Didn't the designers know that the lightweight plastic mailers would function like a sail?

Having to pick them up from the floor was one of the worst parts of the job. Not even Arnold Schwarzenegger who likes to talk about the benefits of working out early in the morning did squats at 3:00 a.m.

I also saw a problem with the way the boxes were sealed at the fulfillment centers. In contrast to Fedex who required that all packages were sealed with the H-tape method, meaning that all the flaps of the box got sealed, the associates who packaged items at Amazon's fulfillment centers only ran a strip of tape over the top of the package and another one over the bottom, presumably to save time.

This method was completely insufficient for sealing flat, oversized boxes. Many of them broke open on the conveyor. Though our problem solvers taped them shut again they wouldn't use heavy-duty tape but cheap packaging tape. Was this Jeff Bezos' idea of "frugality," one of his leadership principles?

And, who decided which kind of cardboard boxes had to be used at the fulfillment centers? Had these people ever heard of 2 and 3-ply cardboard boxes? 1-ply cardboard boxes like the ones Amazon Logistics used aren't designed to hold content heavier than 30 pounds, yet, every day I saw 1-ply boxes that contained 40 to 49 pounds of goods.

Lastly, why didn't we have a trainer team which presented best practices for stowing and also enforced that people would use them?

At Amazon's warehouses, all new associates were trained by one of the learning ambassadors and the facility's learning coordinator. At DSC3, each of them taught what they thought to be the best method, which wasn't necessarily the same method. As far as I knew, none of them had any background in education or corporate training which became very obvious when one checked the new employees' work – all of them did something different.

- 19 -

Naturally, Amazon's customers noticed some of these problems too. A few weeks after I started working at DSC3, one of my author friends posted a picture of her latest shipment from Amazon on Facebook. The box was torn up and had broken open on one side. By the time I saw her posting, it had received more than two dozen comments, including "I have received them in similar fashion" and "Oh good grief. There's no excuse for something like this."

I hated seeing such postings. They always left me embarrassed. What would my friend say if she knew that I worked for the company who sent this package? And, what would I say if she asked me if this package reflected Amazon's concept of "customer obsession"?

This feeling of embarrassment was completely new to me. After Florian died, I learned very quickly, that being a single, widowed mom included that I had to do things I never thought I would have to do, ever. Like having to work two jobs to afford a short camping trip with my children. Or, vacuuming FedexKinkos' store every evening, after I figured out that this would lead to me accruing overtime. (Unfortunately, this gig lasted only four weeks until my manager noticed.) But, never, ever did I feel embarrassed by the quality of work a company I worked for put out. Now – I was. In fact, for this reason, I only told my family and my five closest friends that I worked at Amazon Logistics.

I also felt annoyed. Issues like boxes not getting sealed properly were completely unnecessary. A few feet of heavy-duty tape and allocating an additional 30 seconds per package would solve all problems.

Regardless of the angle from which I looked at these questions, I saw a huge disconnect between Amazon's boasting statements about their "obsession" with customers and Amazon Logistics' way of doing things. Even worse, I also could not escape being reminded of this disconnect every day.

Not only was DSC3 plastered with signs about "customer obsession," right next to the entrance door stood a sign that featured Jeff Bezos' slogan about every day being "Day 1."

This slogan was supposed to express Bezos' business philosophy: That, to be successful, companies needed to maintain the first-day mindset of a start-up. That always challenging the status quo was necessary because doing things "the way they have always been done" would lead to the "death" of a business. It is a philosophy that probably works for most of Bezos' enterprises but not for what we did.

Challenging the law of gravity does not make sense. Hence, putting any kind of goods weighing 40 to 50 pounds into a 1-ply cardboard box that was also sealed insufficiently was, at best, amateurish and, at worst, a safety hazard.

Which was why, for me, the sign said, "It's still Day 1. We are just learning what we want to be doing."

Naturally, I also contemplated if, maybe, by chance, I worked at Amazon's worst ranked warehouse but concluded that this was impossible. The majority of problems did not originate at DSC3. We did not pack anything into boxes or lightweight plastic mailers; all we did was to sort and distribute the goods. Beyond that, it seemed to me that DSC3's management just didn't want to "rock the boat" – in their own interest.

Starting October, it was Peak Season for Amazon.com. Since "forcing" associates to adhere to the guidelines of stowing might lead to associates quitting, the managers just looked away and let the experienced stowers deal with the mess some of the temp workers created, which was exactly what Amazon Logistics did – to them, their managers. For example, Amazon Logistics had to know that the white-blue mailers were too light. Every day, the big fans at the warehouse blew dozens of mailers off the conveyors next to the dock where the operations manager could observe the problem. Hence some warehouse managers had to have reported the issue.

But – apparently – Amazon Logistics' top managers didn't care that their workers had to pick up the mailers, all night long. After all, it wasn't their backs that hurt. So, they let the managers of the delivery stations deal with the problem – they were the ones who had to replenish the workforce when associates quit because they had enough of this kind of nightly exercise.

Amazon Logistics also chose that same strategy when it came to packaging their merchandise. Their top managers didn't have to worry if 40 to 50 pounds of stuff would crash through the bottom of an insufficiently sealed box and possibly hit their toes. Only the warehouse associates and the drivers did.

All of these actions were the exact opposite of employing best practices. Being a believer in best practices I didn't understand why Amazon Logistics operated their way.

- 20 -

As I pondered these questions, I also wondered why Jeff Bezos wanted to run a logistics division in the first place. Not for nothing is last mile delivery the most expensive and most challenging part of the delivery chain – it involves problems like traffic jams, accidents, road closures, catastrophic weather events, and of course, in their case, maintaining a fleet of tens of thousands of vehicles.

Looking at things from up close I even wondered if, maybe, Amazon was losing money on their transportation division. Their competitors' pricing suggested that possibility.

The United States Postal Service who is not known for price gauging, charges a flat rate of $15.05 for shipping a medium-sized package via their priority mail service. But an Amazon Prime member who ordered one item once per month would get a similar quick service for $9.99, the monthly cost of a Prime membership – 33 percent cheaper.

Moreover, since Amazon's Prime membership allowed for placing multiple orders per month, a buyer who ordered one item per week would "pay" only $2.30 for each of the fifty-two express deliveries. How could this work if Amazon also shipped returns, shipped items that got cancelled while in transit, broke stuff, had to replace stuff, hired and fired on a weekly basis, and did thousands of other costly moves? (The United States Postal Service, Fedex, and UPS did not do any of that.)

Though Jeff Bezos was known for willingly accepting financial losses, typically, he used that strategy when he was working on a takeover, like when he put diapers.com out of business. Supposedly, shutting down that upstart had cost Bezos $100 million.

Did Amazon want to put Fedex or UPS out of business, or – both?

Considering what I saw at DSC3, that idea sounded crazy to me. Maybe, Amazon's customers didn't care if a few of their orders arrived in damaged boxes but surely they wanted their own parcels handled "with utmost care."

Amazon's official version was that they started their logistics division because, in the days before Christmas 2013, a combination of bad weather and an overwhelming surge in last-minute online orders led to a delivery fiasco. But that could not be all of it.

Extreme weather poses the same threat to all delivery services, regardless of who owns the trucks and vans. After winter storm Jonas hit my hometown Greenville, SC in January 2016, many Greenville County roads were impassable for days because of downed trees and powerlines. Undoubtedly, in the future, the ever-growing climate emergency would create more problems of this kind.

To me, the mystery of why Amazon got into the transportation business felt like Houdini's "Vanishing Elephant" act. Obviously, Houdini couldn't really make a 5-ton, 8-foot-tall elephant disappear. But, he was able to create an illusion that made it look like the cabinet into which his elephant went was empty.

I believed that, just like Houdini, Jeff Bezos was very talented in creating illusions. Maybe, he followed some of Sun-Tzu's principles, such as "All warfare is based on deception."

When Bezos founded Amazon he only talked about numbers and categories of books (and maybe selling other products in the future) hence people thought that Bezos' new business was all about competing with Barnes & Noble; that it was about competing with one or more retailers.

But, it probably wasn't. In his 2011 interview with Steven Levy, Bezos revealed (maybe accidentally) that he had been working on the Kindle (which catapulted Amazon into the ranks of publishers) pretty much from the start.

When it came to Amazon's Logistics, Bezos only talked about delivery times which, to me, almost proved that he was hiding something. Because transportation isn't only about speed of delivery, it's also about keeping the cargo safe. Hence, maybe, setting up Amazon Logistics was not only about transporting merchandise but about some other goal, just as founding Amazon wasn't only about selling books.

And, just like Houdini's elephant, this other goal was probably hiding in plain sight.

- 21 -

Right then, in time before the Christmas holidays, I was still busy updating my kitchen and my bathroom. These weren't big renovations, but I painted the walls and purchased a few new items – curtains, towels, dishes, glassware, and a few gadgets. Strangely enough, whenever I spent time online checking out kitchen and bathroom stuff, I felt that something that I had noticed every day or at least every week had disappeared from the Internet. I didn't know what it was, which irritated me because I felt that, all of a sudden, I was faced with two riddles I could not solve.

The weeks passed. Then, shortly after Veterans Day, I drove to work a bit earlier than usual. As I made my way through Staunton Bridge Road, a rather narrow, not too well-lit road near DSC3, an Amazon tractor-trailer came toward me. It totally surprised me. I had never seen a semi on this road, neither from Amazon nor any other company. This part of Staunton Bridge Road led to the city and away from the Interstate.

As the truck came closer one of the few streetlights shone on its Prime-blue trailer. The Amazon arrow on its side seemed to smile at me. And, that's when it hit me.

This wasn't a semi that pulled a tractor trailer, this was a semi that pulled a billboard, a 53' billboard that said: (Amazon) Prime. In fact, 53' tractor trailers are even bigger than real highway billboards, which are only 48' wide.

OMG. That was it!

Maybe, Amazon started a logistics division so they could run 30,000 tractor trailers featuring 60,000 "moving billboards" across US highways?

If each trailer was seen by only 500 people, running the trucks converted to 15 million "ad-views" – per day.

Even better, instead of asking, "Hey, don't you want to buy this or that product?", like regular ads do, Amazon's moving billboards had a much better marketing message: "See this 3,816 cubic feet trailer? People in your greater neighborhood purchased the stuff that's in here." And, as if that wasn't enough, Amazon's tens of thousands of delivery vans took the company's message into tens of thousands of U.S. neighborhoods.

Certainly, that marketing strategy took the "Keeping up with the Joneses"-factor to a totally new level.

As I thought through the concept, I also remembered what it was that had disappeared from the Internet – Amazon ads on Facebook.

While working on my renovations, I had looked at hundreds of items at many online stores. In return, all retailers whose products I looked at showed me online ads, trying to sway me to buy their products. All but – Amazon.

My brain was spinning.

Facebook ads cost between seventy cents and ten dollars per click. If, every day, only one million people clicked an Amazon ad at the cost of one dollar, these ads would cost $1 million. Hence, not having to buy ads saved Amazon at least $1 million per day.

Meanwhile I arrived at DSC3. Still having a bit of time before start-of-work, I stayed in my car and checked out Amazon's S-Team. According to his Linkedin profile, in February 2018, Neil Lindsey who had been Amazon's Vice President of Worldwide Marketing became Amazon's Vice President of Worldwide Prime and Marketing.

In other words, in 2018, Amazon.com Inc. put their marketing and Amazon Prime under one hat, which probably meant that it didn't matter whether Amazon's shipping operations were in the red or in the black; Amazon could probably categorize at least part of their trucking operation's costs as marketing and advertising expenditures.

This was not what I expected and at the same time it also was. I always assumed that Jeff Bezos' motivation had to be something bigger and better than making money of shipping merchandise or picking a fight with Fedex and the U.S. Postal Service.

Nobody in their right mind tried to ship cheap *and* fast. The U.S. Postal Service's mission was to "provide the nation with reliable, affordable, universal mail service" to every smallest of small villages in the entire United States of America. And FedEx's mission was to "produce superior financial returns for its shareowners by providing high value-added logistics and transportation..."

Both, the U.S. Postal Service and Fedex were founded in 1971. They knew a thing or two about what could go wrong when transporting packages. Delivering cheap *and* fast was not possible.

Hence, if that's what Amazon said they wanted to do they had to have another reason for why they wanted to be a player in the transportation industry.

Maybe that reason was to use their vehicles as marketing tools?

- 22 -

Oh, what I would have given for being a fly on the wall when somebody at Amazon said, "What if we stop buying ads on social media and run our own ads – on 53' billboards that will be seen by millions of people? All we need to do is – set up our own logistics division with our own semis and our own trailers. This will also help us to compete with Walmart and their semis."

The boldness of this idea was breathtaking. Plus, I was extremely pleased that, apparently, Amazon decided to stop spending marketing dollars on Facebook. I did not like Facebook for a variety of reasons, from their involvement in the 2016 elections to their recurring Internet privacy issues. Every time they got caught, they apologized, saying they could and should do better. In my opinion, this excuse gets old very quickly.

And so, I rededicated myself to Amazon Logistics' mission. If there was a great concept to be discovered like what the original Amazon, the one I fell in love with, did, I wanted to learn more about it.

By now I was a valued member of the stowing team because, most often, my name was #3 on "the list." Once or twice when both of our best stowers took the same day off I even came in as #1. Even the assistant shift manager who didn't seem to like me when I started working at DSC3 made it a point to greet me first whenever she saw me.

Since the job training at DSC3 was still as subpar as it always was, if not worse, some of the new stowers began seeking advice from me; they wanted to know how they could boost their numbers. Naturally, I was always happy to help. Since DSC3's management steadfastly refused to assign specific aisles to each stower, the worst stowers' work affected everybody else's.

Then, one night, a desperate looking young woman approached me, "Hey, Gis, what do you do that you scored 487 today? I never hit a number higher than 260. Please help me. I need this job."

I smiled at her and said, "No problem. Are you placing the jiffies on top of the boxes? If you don't, most likely, you'll struggle with them for the rest of the night."

She looked at me with a surprised look, as if I had asked her if she could speak Mandarin Chinese.

"On top of the boxes? Are you kidding me? Just look at me."

Not knowing what I was looking for I scanned her from head to toe. Ouch! This girl was 5-3 (63 inches), at best.

Whereas I, at 5-8 (68 inches), could easily reach the bags on the fourth tier, 60 to 80 inches above the floor, clearly, she could not. And, probably, all other associates who were 5-6 or shorter struggled with the same issue.

Finally, I found an explanation for why some stowers placed all items along the front edge of the bags on the fourth tier instead of pushing them all the way to the back of the bags. Also, shorter stowers were literally unable to put jiffies on top of boxes on the fourth tier because they could not even reach these spaces! Though DSC3 offered step ladders, hardly anybody used them, probably because getting a step ladder from the end of the aisle cost valuable time.

To me, this was crazy. If Amazon really wanted to hire pretty much everybody who applied for a warehouse job, why didn't they create a setting that allowed all associates to be their best? Like raising the bottom row of bags six inches off the floor so tall people like me wouldn't have to strain their lower backs as they bent down 200 to 300 times per night. Plus, setting up only three rows of shelves elevated by 6 inches would still be only 66 inches high.

This realization encouraged me to mention three or four ideas to my manager about how we at DSC3 could improve our work processes. However, though the manager seemed to be very interested, he did not test any of them.

His reaction did not discourage me; instead, I assumed that my ideas were not bold enough, like what I thought that Amazon's leadership did – forming a logistics company to eliminate the need for online ads. Since by now, Amazon hired and trained new seasonal workers every week, they would probably adopt only a very best idea – a method that could be described in one single sentence.

If only I could only come up with such a method. For sure, that would help me climb the ranks at Amazon Logistics; at least, a little bit.

- 23 -

Soon thereafter, Amazon's (Holiday) Peak 2019 took off. Though DSC3's beautiful break room got decorated with an amazing 3D cardboard fireplace prop and a Christmas tree, somehow the spirit of the season was hard to come by. At Amazon, this season was all about "peaks" – peak numbers of shipments, peak stowing rates, and peak performances.

I fondly remembered the purple Santa hat I received at Fedex where, during Christmas season, we used to call ourselves Santa's little helpers. Even after I left Fedex I wore that thing every Christmas season until it fell apart.

At DSC3, nobody referred to themselves as elves. Most associates only talked about dealing with the enormous volume of work, the additional hours they took on, and the extra money they hoped to make. One associate asked me if I knew if overtime was taxed at a higher rate. I did not. Since DSC3 offered only 6-hour shifts it was extremely difficult to accumulate overtime hours.

Amazon Logistics did not allow their associates to work more than six days per week, which amounted to working 36 hours if one worked only one's regular shift. Hence, the only way to work more than 40 hours per week was to accept double shifts. Which meant – napping in your car between shifts, during wintertime.

Then again, it was pretty obvious that Amazon Logistics tried to avoid having to pay for overtime hours as much possible. They wanted their associates to "work their hardest." To encourage their associates to do so, Amazon Logistics ran competitions called "power hours."

Held at 3:00 a.m. almost every night during Peak 2019, the power hour was Amazon Logistics' equivalent of the Olympics. The stower who stowed the most items during this period won an Echo Dot, a tablet, or a gift card. All others got nothing, not even an honorable mention.

Learning about this competition I was dumbstruck. One of Amazon's claims to fame is that they are a leader in data analysis. Hence, how come that their logistics arm did not see that they themselves gave their stowers the data which showed that, for most of the stowers, it made no sense to compete.

Obviously, stowers whose names were listed in the lower half of "the list" knew that they had zero chances of winning.

For example, the 5 foot 3 girl who made me aware that shorter stowers had problems reaching the bags on the top row of the stowing racks would have had to stow an additional 227 packages just to catch up with me. But there were at least two stowers at DSC3 who stowed even faster than I did, every day of the week.

To encourage participation in their competition DSC3 (or Amazon Logistics) needed to pick a realistic, doable goal. Plus, they needed to add a fun factor. Some element of chance that made people think they could win, just like the lottery.

For example, DSC3 could have announced that the stower who stowed the number of items closest to 327 would win a prize. Which would have prompted all stowers who could stow more than 285 packages per hour to think that they had a shot at winning. For sure, they would have participated if the less than a handful of associates who could hit more than 350 would not have an advantage.

To keep the contest engaging and exciting, the managers could pick a different number every day.

Wasn't all this obvious?

In my opinion, Amazon Logistics' leadership had to know. Literally every public school, YMCA summer camp, and Boys' and Girls Scouts' meeting held games based on this concept.

Aside from all that, the entire concept of the "power hour" seemed wrong to me. At the time, the company did not even offer health insurance to the associates who worked at their delivery stations. And, still, Amazon Logistics aimed to get a good number of their employees to strain themselves even more while "paying/rewarding" only one person with – an in-house product. *(How about a coupon for a deep-tissue massage?)*

I decided that everything about this competition was so odd that I should not offer my ideas. More than likely, DSC3 did not even want any suggestions or advice. When I applied for the position of learning coordinator a few weeks earlier they did not even interview me though I was probably the only candidate with actual teaching experience, managerial experience, and lots of experience in the transportation industry.

If I still wanted to believe that Amazon Logistics was a highly efficient organization, I had to conclude that the power hour was not about raising target rates or processing many more shipments but about something else. Maybe this competition was a disguised psychological endurance test, designed to reveal who of Amazon Logistics' workers would follow every directive including trying to tackle goals they knew they could not achieve?

- 24 -

Finding a perfect stowing tip was much harder than designing a good competition because there were so many variables.

Naturally, all associates had different motivations for working at DSC3. Some did not care where they worked as long as it wasn't in a retail store or in the fast-food industry. Others just wanted to make a quick buck.

There were also mothers who wanted to work at night so they could spend more time with their children, "older" people who couldn't find a job in their industries, students who needed to make money on the side, self-employed who wanted to have a guaranteed income stream, and at least three people who had worked in the transportation industry before and hoped to advance their ambitions.

Though I tried very hard to find the one tip all of them could relate to, I just couldn't do it.

It wasn't the actual work that made me feel brain-dead but the mere view of walls and walls of boxes. Every night of Peak 2019, I walked into aisles whose baker's racks were so fully loaded with packages that I could not even spot the tiniest bit of a picker's bright yellow safety vest on the other side of the walls.

I kept up my morale by telling myself that if Andy Dufresne could tunnel his way out of Shawshank State Penitentiary, most certainly, I could take down these walls of boxes. But, as soon as I removed enough items that a bigger hole appeared the pickers "patched the wall" with more packages.

Even after Christmas the volume of shipments did not decrease right away, and so it took me till mid-February until this strange fog in the color of cardboard, which smothered every intelligent thought, lifted off my brain.

As soon as my mind was clear, I realized what I did wrong during Peak 2019. When trying to come up with a best stowing tip I focused solely on finding a common denominator among DSC3's workforce when really all I needed to do was to focus on the biggest problem.

This realization came as a shock. For decades, I made myself a name as a problem solver but in this instance I failed at applying even basic concepts. Having recovered from Peak Season, my "amazing one sentence tip" came to me almost immediately. Of course, I already knew DSC3's biggest problem – I called it the "jiffy problem."

Because most of the seasonal workers laid the jiffies flat at the bottom of the bags, all stowers were forced to lift boxes on top of the jiffies instead of sliding them into the bags.

This led to three problems. Performing the unusual move many hundreds of times per night caused upper arm pain for the stowers. Also, goods that were bagged in jiffies which ended up below heavier boxes could get damaged. Lastly: Because the bags did not get filled as tight as Amazon's computer system planned, the stowers were forced to waste time closing bags and opening new ones, which led to overtime work.

Therefore, stopping stowers from laying jiffies flat into bags would benefit the stowers, Amazon's customers, and DSC3's management.

Because the shorter stowers were physically unable to place all jiffies on top of the boxes, the only logical solution was to place the jiffies upright into the bags, the same way as the boxes. The only problem with this solution was that the ultralight white-blue plastic mailers were thin, soft, and bendable. They did not stand upright on their own.

So? How does one ensure that thin, soft, and bendable items keep standing? – By using a bookend!

Of course, we didn't have bookends at the warehouse, but we had plenty of small, weighty boxes that could be used like bookends.

This method could also be described in one sentence: "Instead of laying jiffies flat at the bottom of the bags we want you to stand all envelopes upright – like books – and secure them with a package that you use like a bookend." Out. Over. Everybody could envision the process and everybody could do it, including shorter people.

I was exhilarated. Ignoring what my friend said months ago, I now felt certain that finding this easy-to-do stowing tip would help me in advancing my career at Amazon Logistics. Because solving this problem equated to solving three problems at once.

A few days later, I had the opportunity to introduce my idea to the manager.

"Like a bookend?" he said. "Yeah, that's good. Have you applied for problem solver already?"

"Thank you," I said. "Yes, I applied, sometime in November."

"Well, why don't you fill out the application again. We'll nominate new problem solvers in about four to five weeks."

- 25 -

Now that things were quieter at DSC3 I needed to take off a few days – I wanted to visit my family in Vienna, Austria because my dad died somewhat unexpectedly before the Christmas holidays.

Right then, at the beginning of March 2020, Covid-19 was thought of as "a kind of flu" in the United States. Still, trying to be prepared for all eventualities, I purchased five boxes of N95 face masks (50 pieces) before I left for Vienna.

Much to my surprise, as soon as I arrived there, I found out more about Amazon's inner workings.

Two days into my vacation, I received an "attendance check-in"-email from Amazon-HR asking me if I was no longer interested in working for the company and if I wished to submit my resignation. I immediately replied, telling Amazon-HR that I booked my vacation on their scheduling app AtoZ and asked to check it there. I also copied DSC3's local HR person who also contacted HR-Attendance and asked them not to terminate me, because she and both my managers knew that I traveled to Europe for a family visit. Her email got acknowledged.

Most astoundingly, within the next six days I received two more "courtesy outreach"-emails asking me if I quit. Realizing that these emails couldn't possibly have been sent by a thinking person but were sent by some kind of time clock autoresponder, I googled the turn-over rate of Amazon Logistics' associates. In 2017, it was 100.9 percent. *Wow! I didn't know that.*

Unfortunately, by the time I returned to the United States the Covid-19 situation had turned into a full-blown crisis. With it began a period in which I finally realized that Amazon was no longer the company I admired for more than twenty years.

Returning to work on March 15, I could only work the first session, inducting jiffies instead of stowing. Then, the assistant shift manager sent me home to self-quarantine for two weeks. So, I stayed home and spring-cleaned my home and yard.

By the time I returned to work again, DSC3 had rolled out Amazon's Covid-19 Safety Initiative. While we had no shortages of PPEs, the policy which according to the Centers for Disease Control and Prevention (CDC) was most important, was getting violated in plain sight.

Though all employees dutifully put on face masks when entering the building, already half-an-hour later a third of them wore their masks below their noses. After lunch, that number increased to forty percent and during the last work session to sixty percent.

Obviously, this was a serious problem. DSC3 is not a nice, air-conditioned office or retail store but a warehouse where people move packages weighing up to 50 pounds. Naturally, people who work that hard also breathe harder and people who wear their face masks below their noses breathe harder through their noses.

That situation became outright dangerous when pickers who did not wear their masks correctly placed a heavy package on a baker's rack. Obviously, like every normal person they exhaled as they put the package on the rack.

But these racks were only 2 feet wide!

This meant that the pickers were within 2 feet of the stowers who had to get a new package from the rack every 12 seconds, all night long.

Amazon Logistics' leadership had to know that. Or did they not know the dimensions of the equipment they acquired?

Still, I never saw anybody walking around and reminding the pickers to pull up their masks.

Though, at first, I was extremely annoyed with the fact that many of my colleagues were not wearing their masks correctly, I quickly figured out why they did not mask up – it was getting hot at the warehouse! Warehouses whose bay doors get opened frequently are hard to keep cool.

By summer, it was so hot that management posted reminders to stay hydrated to avoid having a heatstroke. Plus, on most days, the problem solvers brought the associates cold water so they would not forget to drink plenty of cool fluids. Naturally, having to wear a face-mask in this type of environment added to the general discomfort.

As always, there would have been creative options for attempting to solve the issue. For example, DSC3's management could have decided that, every week, they'd raffle off three swag items among the people who never got caught not wearing their mask the proper way.

Unfortunately, our managers did not explore any such options; they were preoccupied with dealing with the immense volume of work as well as trying to hire people who would not quit within days.

Moreover, in early April, it became apparent that Amazon was in trouble. In contrast to the "fake review crisis" which aggravated only Amazon authors and vendors, this time around, large segments of the U.S. population and even the world were affected. On social media platforms, customers vented that they did not get their orders within the promised two days and in ecommerce forums vendors complained that Amazon stopped accepting their shipments of non-essential goods. For the first time, "the world" realized what enormous power Amazon wields and what happens if Amazon is not prepared to address a specific problem.

- 26 -

Looking at the bigger picture, it appeared to me that Amazon Logistics attacked the Covid-19 crisis in the same manner Amazon executives seemed to attack every crisis or inconvenience. They threw money at the problem and touted their own horn.

When, in April 2020, the media was tipped off about health concerns at Amazon warehouses, Amazon stated that they were taking "extreme measures" to ensure the safety of their employees. To back up that claim they peppered their employees, their customers, their investors, journalists, and politicians with imposing numbers – the hundreds of millions of dollars they spent, the millions of facemasks they delivered, the thousands of handwashing stations and thermal cameras they added, and so on, without ever admitting that, indeed, there were problems.

In fact, Amazon used one of the oldest marketing tricks to make their actions look as impressive as possible. Instead of saying they handed out x number of bottles of hand sanitizer, Amazon described the effort as "providing 48 million ounces" of hand sanitizer.

But, while they did all of this and more, they were unable to ensure the most important preventive measure – that all their warehouse employees wore their facemasks properly.

It could have been easy to achieve that. If one wants to accomplish a specific goal, it helps to call things what they are, or what they should be.

Hence, if Amazon had decided to pay their workers a "facemask wearing compensation" instead of paying hazard pay and a bonus, they would have "established a kind of contract" every employee understood – "You wear your facemask properly and we'll pay you for doing it."

Taking this radical step would have also helped with worker retention, raised Amazon Logistics' image as an employer, and, possibly, suppressed efforts to unionize.

By admitting that their workers deserved at least an additional $2 per hour for wearing a facemask while lifting or pushing boxes up to 50 pounds in close to 80 degrees heat, Amazon might also have helped their customers to feel better about ordering from them.

In my opinion, it was Amazon's chance to, once again, become the company whose praise people shouted from the rooftops, like independent authors and small publishers used to do during Amazon's early days.

But Amazon did not take it. Instead, they became the company whose chairman's wealth increased by $74 billion to an astounding $175 billion, within six months, while Amazon associates toiled in hot warehouses.

Not surprisingly, in his annual letter to shareholders, Jeff Bezos too touted Amazon's "extreme measures" but he also mentioned that training the new hires with distancing requirements was "challenging." The way I saw it, Amazon Logistics' "frugal shortcuts" came to haunt them, all the way. Just like any crisis in history, the Covid-19 crisis laid bare preexisting problems.

Because Amazon Logistics didn't use the most excellent video courses to train their new employees, they didn't have the best educational tools to fall back on. Because they also did not hire professional trainers but had their learning coordinators (problem solvers) teach the new employees, these "untaught teachers" were not prepared to teach people plagued by economic worries. And, because hands-on peer education, previously an integral part of training, became impossible due to social distancing, experienced associates could not help the new employees like they used to do. At DSC3, all of this did not go well.

When, after returning from Europe, I saw the new stowers' work for the first time, I was literally speechless. Every bag contained a jumble of jiffies and boxes. Also, my "bookend tip" had not been implemented. Naturally, the latter was disappointing to me, but I always knew that this idea was not the only solution to dealing with the problem.

The real shock came when I had an opportunity to observe the new hires getting trained in early April 2020. It made me feel as if I was watching a low-budget home movie.

To ensure social distancing, the new hires stood on floor markers in front of a model baker's rack in a corner of the warehouse. The instructor stood next to the rack and gestured at the bags while holding a lengthy speech. I watched them for a minute or two while questioning what I was doing at a place like this.

Was I imagining this?

The world's second most-admired company operated on the level of the little red schoolhouse? Really, the only thing that was missing from that scene was a long pointer.

Amazon owns movie studios. Even if they didn't have excellent educational videos, why didn't they follow their leadership principle "Be biased for Action" and immediately create something fitting to their status? All they needed to do was to tell one of their movie artists to create a short video with computer generated imagery of boxes and jiffies "flying into the bags" the way they should be stowed. Why on Earth didn't they do that? Since Amazon's movie artists could not work because the movie industry had to shut down, this would have been a perfect time to create this kind of videos.

The moment reshaped my view of Amazon: Never mind what Jeff Bezos and official Amazon Logistics voices proclaimed, for me it was no longer possible to see the company as the dynamic innovator they claimed to be.

At DSC3, the result of Amazon Logistics' unenthusiastic way of training their new employees was a chaotic work climate.

New employees who hoped to turn their temporary jobs into permanent positions tried to make rate by putting or even throwing small packages and jiffies into the bags, without following any system, which made work harder for all of us. Many experienced associates stayed home for weeks or quit altogether. My three best friends and one of the two best stowers also left. And I myself pondered quitting too.

Then, out of the blue (or as a result of the Covid-19 crisis), the company decided to offer their experienced associates health insurance if they committed to working an additional six hours per week.

So, I figured it'd be best to stay until the unemployment rate dipped below 10 percent. I also spent $190 on a top-of-the-line envomask ® with soft AIRgel cushion, plus enough spare filters to keep me safe for the next three months.

- 27 -

Considering the Covid-related chaos, I should have known that it was only a matter of time until I came across additional problems but, never in my life, would I have guessed that I would encounter – money issues.

Amazon Logistics offered two options of unpaid-time-off – UPT (Unpaid-Time-Off) and VTO (Voluntary-Time-Off). The most important difference between UPT and VTO was that UPT was measured in full hours, whereas VTO was counted in minute increments.

VTO was the warehouse managers' spiel. They offered VTO when they wanted to send one or more employees home, so Amazon Logistics could save payroll.

On the other hand, UPT could be taken by the associates. Every quarter, Amazon gave every associate 20 hours of UPT, which they could use to cover sick time or emergencies or accrue the time for a few days of unpaid vacation. UPT also had a darker element: Employees who clocked in more than 5 minutes late or clocked out more than 5 minutes early were "charged" a full hour of UPT.

In practical terms, this meant that an employee who accepted VTO 10 minutes before the end of their shift got paid for the 50 minutes they worked before they left, whereas an employee who "skipped out" 10 minutes early did not get paid for the 50 minutes they worked. To ensure that Amazon's time clock system registered VTOs correctly, employees had to have their badges scanned by one of the managers.

Obviously, once the Covid crisis began, this system became unusable. At the onset of the crisis, Amazon needed to offer their warehouse employees a way to stay home for much longer than the time they had accrued so they could take care of their school-aged children or elderly relatives. Hence, Amazon "turned off" their UPT-VTO system and offered unlimited unpaid-time-off. But, at Amazon, nothing lasts forever and, on May 1, 2020, they "switched back" to their UPT-VTO system so all associates would have to return to work.

Three days later, I ran into trouble. When, in the first week of May, I accepted VTO twice, Amazon's AtoZ app recorded both of my VTOs as UPTs. Which meant that unless I took action to get this fixed, I wasn't going to get paid for working 35 minutes and 50 minutes respectively.

Since Amazon has a history of suffering glitches (most recently on Prime Day 2019), I assumed that this problem was caused by a glitch which happened when Amazon added numerous Covid-related resources to their AtoZ app.

I also assumed that my problem would get corrected immediately. After all, it was Covid-crisis days and Amazon aired "Thank You, Heroes"-commercials on social media telling "the world" how much they valued their employees and their work.

So, I emailed Human Resources screen-prints of my time sheets as well as the names of the two assistant shift managers who offered the VTOs and asked HR to correct my time sheet.

But, while in the real world "outside of Amazon," most HR persons would have responded with, "Thank you for sending this information, I'll verify and get back to you," that did not happen at Amazon.

Instead, an Amazon HR-person reminded me that UPT is taken for "any clock out earlier than 5 minutes" and that therefore they could not refund me.

I was in shock. Firstly, about how I got treated by my employer who, after all, asked me if I wanted to go home early so the company could save payroll and then about the possibility that HR didn't seem to realize that they had a problem on their end.

On the day, when I VTOed the second time, the assistant shift manager offered VTO because the last truck was late and there was no work. Quite a few associates accepted VTO and stood in line with me while we waited to get our badges scanned. Hence, I wondered if their absences were recorded as VTOs or UPTs.

It didn't take long until I heard of problems. For some of DSC3's employees having or not having every penny of their paycheck made a difference.

All I could think was, "Really, Amazon? That's how you treat your 'heroes'?"

Still, I wasn't going to go after HR because as a former project manager I could envision the situation they were in. Most likely, their department was a zoo. They were busy hiring 100,000 people.

What I could not understand was that the HR's leadership team did not foresee that a glitch might happen and instruct their personnel accordingly.

Everybody who followed Amazon – buyers, vendors, and indie authors – knew that Amazon's site experienced glitches in regular intervals. The Prime Day glitches of 2016, 2018, and 2019 made headline news around the world.

So, why did Amazon's leadership not play "the safe card" and come up with a sensible plan for what to do if adding dozens of Covid-related resources to their AtoZ app plus adding an additional 100,000 new employee-users caused a glitch?

Telling employees who drudged away in hot warehouses while also worrying they might get infected with a potentially life-threatening virus that they would not get paid for the time they worked seemed like the worst idea anybody could come up with.

It was also an insanely unproductive strategy. Obviously, warehouse associates who did not get paid had to shift their problem to their managers, thereby occupying their time too with addressing issues that should not have occurred in the first place.

The easiest way to deal with these problems would have been to tell the Human Resources team, "If, for whatever reason, an associate complains about a glitch, pay them for every minute they worked. Right now, we need our associates more than ever."

Alas, it seemed that Amazon did not consider any of these thoughts. They aired "Thank You, Heroes"-commercials and did what they always did.

All these led me to think that for all of Jeff Bezos' efforts to emphasize the importance of his "Day-1"-philosophy (including setting up stand-up floor signs in front of warehouses) it appeared that Amazon Logistics had become the embodiment of what Bezos' "Day 1"-philosophy warned about – an uncreative behemoth that did things "the way they always did."

In the end, it took four weeks and two emails from my manager until I got paid for 65 minutes but not for all 85 minutes.

Meanwhile, Amazon made more than $4 billion in profit, in the second quarter of 2020.

- 28 -

But, while, in the past, not getting paid correctly would have majorly upset me, in May 2020 it did not. And that was because I was depressed. Though, for the second time in this century I avoided disaster – I was gainfully employed while the unemployment rate soared to double digits – this time, I did not feel good about where I was. There was no lying about it – I was stuck in a dead-end employment.

In the nine months I worked at DSC3 I applied for the in-house positions of learning coordinator, problem solver (twice), and, most recently, for one of seven seats on DSC3's new safety commission. Though I was more than qualified for each position and also hit DSC3's target rate almost every day, I did not get any of these minor promotions.

Especially, not getting a seat on the safety commission was a slap in the face. Of all associates working at DSC3 I was most likely the one who cared the most about safety issues. However, the person or group who chose the members of the safety commission indicated that, in their opinion, I was not even the seventh most qualified candidate.

It was therefore painfully obvious that DSC3 (or Amazon Logistics) did not want me to move up though I contributed plenty of helpful ideas that shed light on my qualifications.

On top of giving the manager "my bookend"-tip, in April 2020, I also delivered an assessment of how the condition of our finger scanners affected DSC3's work output. Nobody asked me to do that; I just did because I noticed that nobody else was looking into the issue.

By April, some of the finger scanners performed so sluggish that using one of the worn scanners I scanned 40 fewer items per hour than if I used one of the better ones. On top of that, regularly having to use a bad scanner caused an inflammation of my right thumb joint, a form of carpal tunnel syndrome.

"We might have to replace the five or six worst scanners," I suggested to the manager. "The numbers add up. 5 times 40 scans times 6 hours equals 1,200. So, during every shift, we lose between 1,000 to 1,200 scans."

At every other company, taking initiative, researching, and analyzing this type of information would have led to some positive consequences. But, it did not at DSC3 (or Amazon Logistics); not even when I did not talk about my hurting thumb but about the company's favorite topic – their numbers.

Which made it crystal clear that I was working for the wrong company.

Still, it was my own fault that I was in this situation.

Warned again and again that Amazon was not what they appeared to be, I had nothing better to do than ignore what the broker, the printer, and my friend at DSC3 told me, plus myriads of newspaper and magazine articles.

Oddly enough, it was the articles that suggested to me that I would do well working at Amazon, even though they described Amazon warehouses as "bruising workplaces" (New York Times) with "grueling working conditions" (The Guardian).

For some crazy reason, I believed that a company that demanded obligatory excellence from their "lowliest employees" had to be even more excellent themselves.

But, instead of spotting amazing excellence, I found an outdated trainings program, an ill-designed award program, insufficient boxes and packaging tape, shelves that made it hard for shorter people to do their job, and what looked like total unwillingness to correct deficiencies, all in favor of "taking things day by day" and "getting the employees to do what it takes to hit the numbers."

In my opinion, Amazon.com Inc. had no love for Amazon Logistics.

Of course, I could have and should have researched this information before I applied at DSC3, but I didn't.

And that was, because for more than twenty years, I did what I now considered as "drinking Jeff Bezos' Kool-Aid."

I believed Bezos' message that Amazon "thought big" and was "biased for action," aimed to "hire and develop the best" and "insisted on the highest standards" because they wanted to "learn and be curious", "dive deep" and "invent and simplify" so they could "have backbone; disagree and commit" and "be right, a lot," which, inevitably, would lead to that they "owned" their work and "delivered results" to "earn trust" and live up to their promise of "customer obsession." Unfortunately, what I found was mostly – uninspiring (instead of clever) "frugality."

Could I muster the strength to leave this place in the midst of a pandemic? The U.S. unemployment rate still stood at 13 percent and my home state's unemployment rate was the highest since record keeping began.

And so, I stayed.

- 29 -

Then, at the beginning of May, an unexpected, mind-boggling, unheard-of event happened. I found out about it while socially distancing in my car during the late-night lunch break.

Tim Bray, VP and Distinguished Engineer at Amazon webservices, resigned over Amazon firing whistleblowers who protested working conditions at Amazon's warehouses. Reading Bray's blog, I was touched. This former Amazon executive cared about people, the environment, the principle of things and – he stood up for all three.

In his blog, Tim Bray also spoke of "a vein of toxicity" running through the company culture. *Whoa – one of Amazon's bosses articulated what I thought?*

Bray's stunning move was the latest in a series of events concerning Amazon's dealings with Covid-related problems. About a month earlier, Amazon fired Chris Smalls, one of their management assistants and the organizer of a strike at Amazon's warehouse JFK8. Only days later, a leaked memo revealed how Amazon wanted to deal with the situation.

David Zapolsky, Amazon's general counsel, suggested to focus on laying out a case for why Smalls' actions were unacceptable, so Amazon would be "...in a much stronger PR position..." and could "... follow with their usual talking points..."

This was precisely what I now perceived to be Amazon's "vein of toxicity." In my opinion, the company worried mostly about their PR position and about opportunities to repeat their talking points; the latter being Amazon's PR 2.0.

Coming back from Europe, I myself complained about the facemask problem. But, all I got was Amazon's talking point – "We are taking everybody's temperature as soon as they enter the building."

And, when I countered that the digital thermometer did not even work properly because it said, that my body temperature was 94.1, I got to hear, "We'll be getting a noncontact infrared thermometer camera any day."

And, when I countered this argument by saying, that considering that people could be asymptomatic carriers, it was more important that everybody wore their facemasks properly, I received a reply which seemed to ignore the urgency of the problem – "We are auditing the facility to evaluate the issue."

What was there to audit? No matter where I was in the warehouse, I could see at least one person who wasn't wearing their facemask properly. Plus, we were talking about potential exposure to an extremely dangerous virus and not about wasting copy paper or some other minor detail.

These one-sided discussions took place after Amazon fired Chris Smalls. Hence, even under the spotlight of the media, apparently, Amazon did not reevaluate their approach to dealing with the problem but kept repeating their "usual talking points."

Then, three weeks later, Tim Bray resigned.

To me, his decisive action felt like a vindication – somebody who was somebody at Amazon.com refused to listen to another round of talking points. How would Amazon react?

Though they could come up with all kinds of explanations for why Chris Smalls organized a protest at JFK8, what could Amazon say about Tim Bray? Since Bray had nothing to gain but everything to lose, it was clear that his voice was impartial.

But – it seemed once again, it was no longer "Day 1" at Amazon. They declined to comment on Bray's sudden departure and that was that.

Their refusal to comment appeared to be another one of their talking points. When I googled the verbatim phrase "Amazon declined to comment," I got more than 460,000 search results.

Thinking through the events it became clear to me that Amazon simply did not appreciate opposing viewpoints. Chris Smalls tried to stand up for his cause and Tim Bray quit because he owned his truth. And I myself identified issues that needed improvement.

Maybe, the reason why I never got promoted was that I was not a yes-girl?

It was easy to feel small when surrounded by Amazon's "Wall of Talking Points."

- 30 -

Two or three weeks later, one of my best friends from Vienna called.

"What's up, Gisela? It's been weeks since you left for USA and I still haven't heard from you. Are you okay?"

That last question hit hard, and I broke down.

"No, I am not," I confessed. "Literally, everything blew up on me." Then, I started telling him that what I had told him in Vienna, namely that I'd get promoted to problem solver, did not happen.

"Wait, wait," my friend interrupted. "I thought you told me that the manager specifically told you to apply for this job because you solved one of their big problems."

"That is correct," I said. "But, apparently, he just teased me. I don't want to bother you with the details. The bottom line is, I am caught in a totally useless employment. Even worse, because of that stupid virus, it's probably not smart to try changing anything about this situation in the next two or three months. In short – I am screwed, and I did it to myself."

"Whew, Gisela, I have never heard you talk like this. You are the girl that can do anything. I remember when I wanted to talk you into coming back to Austria after Florian died. Then I thought your plan to raise your kids in America, alone by yourself, was undoable. But – you did it! You are Miss Invincible."

"Ha," I laughed sarcastically. "Then, we weren't dealing with a highly contagious, nasty virus. And, with 13 percent unemployment. And, with Zoom job interviews, if one can even get an interview. If this Covid-crisis goes on any longer, my career in transportation is dead. Instead of being a transportation specialist with a nice resume I am now a warehouse worker."

I groaned, "I cannot believe that I was so stupid to believe Amazon's talking points."

"Calm down, Gisela, calm down. Never mind what you are working now, you still are a transportation specialist. Is that even what you want to be?"

"Well," I sighed, "Of course, I would have preferred to be a best-selling author. But I like logistics, I really do. It's all about solving problems and I am good at that."

"Gisela," my friend said in his calmest voice. "Maybe that is the problem. Maybe you need to stop trying to solve other people's problems. Do what Bezos does. Focus mostly on what's good for you."

"Ha. Ha. Ha," I bristled. "You are so funny. 'Do what Bezos does?' Have you heard that he is the richest person in this universe? He can do anything he wants to do, including going to Mars."

"Gisela, that's not what I meant. I am telling you to do the right thing for yourself instead of focusing on how you can help Amazon when – apparently – they don't want your help. If Bezos was in your situation, he would not work his butt off for someone else."

"No, he would not. That's for sure."

"Exactly. So, do what he does and focus on what you can do for yourself. Unfortunately, because of Covid, I can't fly to USA and help you but I'll call you next weekend. I promise."

- 31 -

After we hung up, I poured myself a fresh cup of coffee and thought about what my friend said. Of course, he was right. Virus or no virus, just hanging in there and letting life happen was never a great idea. It was also true that, in the past, I never behaved like this. The only reason why I felt paralyzed now was that just hearing the words "double-digit unemployment rate" brought back memories of making it through the Great Recession. At the time, I hoped that I'd never have to experience an event of that magnitude again, yet here we were, living through a pandemic.

Obviously, finding a new job would be difficult. And, even if I landed a job, that employment might not last since the Covid crisis was far from over. Maybe I should follow Steve Jobs' advice "Stay Hungry, Stay Foolish" and make the ultimate "Stay-Hungry-Stay-Foolish"-move – write another book?

The idea had a lot going for it. Writing a book was a great way to kill time alone. I could write a second memoir. But – did I have a story to tell?

During my years working in Austria's movie industry, I worked for a brilliant producer who had a litmus test for deciding which of the scripts he was offered every week he wanted to read. He called the script writers and asked them to sum up their story in one sentence. The producer's concept was simple - "A script can be good or bad, and even a bad script can be turned into a good script. But – if a script doesn't present an idea we care about it will never be a great movie." So, I tried out his concept for my book's idea.

"My memoir tells the story of how I personally experienced Amazon going from most powerful supporter of the First Amendment to a company who just 'spins off' ideas to make money at the expense of others."

I wrote the sentence down, read it, and read it again, and a third time. To me, it sounded like a modern Greek tragedy.

And, in a way, it was. Because I noticed that, in their quest to cope with their business' needs and requirements, Amazon did ugly things, including hurting people who helped them.

For example, during Amazon's early days, when Bezos needed his new ecommerce store to stand out from the crowd of retailers, Amazon courted persons who had the talent to write reviews which Amazon's customers found "helpful." To encourage these elite reviewers to write more reviews – for free – Amazon awarded the best of them with titles like Top-1000 reviewer, Top-100 reviewer, and even Hall-of Fame reviewer.

Not surprisingly, these reviewers enjoyed their newfound influencer status and they loved Amazon. Many of them were retirees who penned upwards of 20,000 reviews, thereby devoting years of their lives to working for Amazon – for free. These persons' reviews not only helped Amazon to sell goods, but also challenged other reviewers to up the level of their book and product reviews.

In my opinion, Amazon's effort to attract these reviewers and get them to write millions of book and product reviews for free was the greatest word-of-mouth marketing campaign in history.

Eventually, when "fake review"-writers threatened to overtake Amazon's review platform, Amazon installed algorithms to find and kick out the cheaters. Rightfully or wrongfully, they also kicked out 29 of 182 Hall-of-Fame reviewers.

But that was not the ugly thing.

Worst of all was that Amazon proceeded in a way that looked like "public shaming" – they announced which of the Hall-of-Famers they kicked out on their Hall-of-Fame Reviewer page.

On that publicly accessible web page which features the names, "recognitions," and number of reviews each Hall-of-Famer wrote, Amazon replaced the demoted reviewers' tally with a glaring comment – "0 reviews," thereby identifying these people who had given them so much as people who, by Amazon's standards, were "review cheaters."

This did not need to be.

If Amazon wanted to kick them out so be it. But why not simply freeze these Hall-of-Famers' review records instead of featuring humiliating "0s"?

Allowing these reviewers to keep a "receipt" for their amazing work, which helped Jeff Bezos to take his business off the ground, was the least Amazon could do. Alas, Amazon chose to simply delete the records of these persons' work thereby throwing away years of their lives and publicly shaming them on top of that.

Then again, more than likely, Jeff Bezos just didn't waste a thought on these people as soon as he did not need them anymore.

This ugly situation was one of the reasons why I stopped thinking of Amazon as a principled business a few years ago, but I always thought of them as an extremely competent organization – until the Covid-crisis took off. Then, it became obvious that the company was not prepared to deal with situations their algorithms could not forecast.

This could be a huge problem if a company seeks world domination, like Amazon seems to do.

I reflected on that thought and decided that, yes – I hadd a story to tell. In fact, there were probably only very few people who had a 22-year story with Amazon like I did.

In 1998, long before Amazon published millions of independent authors' works, I opened a vendor's account on Amazon to sell my self-published book. In 2003, I became a stockholder who lost money and eventually sold my shares. Starting 2012, I published more than a dozen books on their platform, including five books about Amazon's review platform. In 2012, I also began reviewing on Amazon, "serving" as a top-reviewer from 2014 to 2018. Throughout these years, I spent thousands of hours studying everything Amazon did on their review platform. My book, *Naked Truths About Getting Book Reviews* was a Finalist at the coveted Kindle Book Review Awards. Finally, in 2019, I became one of their warehouse associates who got a chance to see Amazon Logistics' operations from up close. In short, I heard and saw stories others never knew about.

Which prompted my next question – Had anybody ever written a book about working at Amazon?

A quick search revealed that British journalist James Bloodworth penned *Hired: Six Months Undercover in Low-Wage Britain* and American journalist Emily Guendelsberger wrote *On the Clock: What Low-Wage Work Did to Me and How It Drives America Insane*. Both books seemed to focus on the abuse of workers at different corporations, including at Amazon.

This was interesting. How did Amazon react to the publication of Guendelsberger's and Bloodworth's books?

Guendelsberger worked for Amazon in 2015 and her book got released in 2019. Bloodworth worked for Amazon in 2016 but his book was released already in 2018. Amazon said about Bloodworth's book that his book was not an "accurate portrayal" and that they no longer used the points system Bloodworth described. And, about Guendelsberger's book they said, that she worked at Amazon for only eleven days, hence – again – that her description of events could not be an "accurate portrayal" of working at one of their warehouses.

This implied that to avoid Amazon attacking me with the same talking points, I would have to keep working at DSC3.

This was a tall order. Working in the logistics industry can be extremely strenuous.

I remembered that Charles Bukowski worked for the post office during his early career. Hence, the real question was – Was I as tough as Charles Bukowski? Probably not, but at least I could try. If there ever was a perfect time to write a book this was it. For sure, the Covid crisis was not going away in the next six months.

- 32 -

The following weekend my Viennese friend called, "How are you doing? Are you in a better mood?"

"Yes," I smiled. "Thank you for your encouraging support. I decided that I am going to write a new memoir, about my two decades of somehow being connected to Amazon."

"That's wonderful. I was hoping that you'd say that because I love your stories. Your *Naked Determination* is such a beautiful book. But – Can you do it? What if Bezos sues you?"

"Heck, no! Bezos can't sue me. I work for Amazon, but that doesn't mean that Bezos owns me.

Of course, I can't reveal any proprietary information, like the number of Covid cases at DSC3 or the number of shipments we process every night, or how many people DSC3 employs, but I don't want to do that anyway. To be honest, I believe that Amazon Logistics' credo 'Don't tell anything' is nonsense by legal standards because they don't tell us anything. Also, DSC3 is not some kind of clandestine enterprise. Nobody who works there drives an Aston Martin."

My friend laughed out loud.

I continued. "Proprietary information is confidential information – like the way Amazon's builds their algorithms, their patents, copyrights, and trademarks. However, anything that's observed by millions of people and is shown on TV and on Youtube, not to talk about Amazon's own PR videos, cannot possibly be regarded a secret. Also, nondisclosure agreements can't protect anything that was disclosed in the past, for example, by a journalist.

Today, all noteworthy U.S. publications except for fashion and home and garden magazines have an 'Amazon reporter,' somebody who reports about 'everything Amazon' from their stock price to their workers' initiatives, their accident rates, and environmental issues, pros and cons. After all, Amazon is a publicly traded company. People want to know what's up. In the last twenty-five years, tens of thousands of articles have been written about Amazon. Plus, there is social media. In these venues thousands of Amazon associates vent about their jobs and, believe me, they reveal a lot about what's going on at their warehouses."

I poured myself another cup of coffee.

"In their non-disclosure agreement, Amazon writes that they consider everything that is not generally known to the public as confidential. But I'd argue that 'the public' is already 'inside Amazon's warehouses.'

Right now, Amazon employs around 700,000 warehouse employees, a group of people larger than the entire population of the states of Wyoming or Vermont. Certainly, 700,000 people are 'the public.' But if one adds all employees who left Amazon or got fired in the last two years as well as all seasonal workers plus the drivers who were or are employed by third party contractors the number of Americans who know precisely what is going inside Amazon's warehouses is probably closer to two million – about 1 percent of adults living in the United States.

No American corporation can tell two million Americans 'You can't talk about what you see here.' That only happens in countries with authoritarian regimes, but not in America, the Land of the Free."

"Right," my friend said. "When I was young, we used to travel a lot to Hungary, Czechoslovakia, and Poland before the Iron Curtain came down."

"Yep, I even traveled Russia three times, and I crossed the country with the Transsib twice. Seven days on the train," I reminisced.

"I am not sure why Amazon states the things they say – some of Amazon's policies are almost comical. For example, in their course about non-disclosure of information, Amazon states that we associates can't tell anybody which items we handle at a higher rate, in other words which items sell best on any given day. This is a crazy statement because Amazon itself gives this information to everybody who wants to know. They have bestseller lists and they also sort their categories by bestselling items. So, what the heck is Amazon talking about when they say that *we* cannot divulge which items sell best on any given day?"

I exhaled with a sigh. "Sometimes, I have the feeling that at Amazon the right hand doesn't know what the left hand is doing. Oh, and by the way, I just discovered that Amazon got infiltrated by two undercover journalists and both of them wrote books about what they saw."

My friend laughed. "You are so clever and so funny. The thought of Amazon workers being clandestine operatives who might drive an Aston Martin like James Bond is very funny."

I giggled too. "Well, that's what happens when Amazon Logistics accidentally hires a person who graduated with a master's degree in film and mass media and who is also a transportation professional."

- 33 -

Sadly, writing my book turned out to be harder than I thought; maybe because I wasn't as tough as Charles Bukowski.

Five days per week, I worked at DSC3 from 10:15 p.m. till 4:45 a.m. Then I slept till noon. Though I hoped that five afternoons and two extra days were plenty of time to write a book, it was not. The Covid crisis did not get any better and DSC3 still operated on "Peak"-levels. On most days, I felt so wiped out that I could not write more than one paragraph; on some days I couldn't even do that.

Hence, when I spotted a DSC3 internal announcement that the warehouse needed to hire an Interim Acting Safety Champion, I decided that I should try one last time to get some kind of promotion and applied for the job.

But, once again, a person who, in the past, helped a NVOCC and freight forwarder to get their C-TPAT certification (Customs Trade Partnership Against Terrorism), who knew a lot about OSHA rules and regulations from her time working at a construction company, and who was known to point out safety issues at DSC3 – me – did not get invited to interview. To say that this was baffling did not even begin to describe what I thought about the experience.

So I did what I should have done a long time ago – I checked out company reviews penned by Amazon warehouse employees.

The company had a ranking of 3.5 out of 5 on Glassdoor and 3.6 out of 5 on Indeed. One of the first reviews I read warned of "false and paid-for reviews" which in the reviewer's opinion were planted by Amazon's PR team.

I could not help but laughing out loud. To me, it was funny finding out that Amazon, of all companies, found themselves "on the other side." Instead of hosting reviews in which reviewers claimed all sorts of things suddenly they were the target of accusations.

As it could be expected, the best reviews came from people who valued that they were paid $15 per hour. Still, even positive reviews mentioned "HR is terrible", "Con: Favoritism," and "They are not enforcing their own Covid policy."

Negative reviews noted below average training, rude managers, and obvious or even blatant favoritism. There were also complaints about insufficient equipment and that Amazon Logistics had a habit of "hiring young college grads" and "overlooking experienced associates."

No kidding! In my case Amazon Logistics overlooked a candidate with years of industry experience, a college grad who had also taken six sigma courses relating to the industry, a former vocational teacher, and bilingual person who had an E.U. passport as well as a U.S. green card.

That alone should be worth gold to an International company like Amazon. Regardless of whether I traveled to Europe or to the United States, I always passed through customs in the fast lane. And yet – most likely, Amazon's managers and HR-people who looked at my resume said, "She isn't twenty-something, and she is not a yes-girl."

Why did I ever think that this company "thought big," in every aspect of their operations?

This too was noted by many reviewers. A surprising number of them mentioned that, at their facilities, Amazon's leadership principles were ignored. Apparently, there was a downside to displaying one's brand message on the lunchroom's walls.

Employees who might have never looked up their employer's leadership principles read them in the breakroom and judged Amazon by what they saw. Some of them articulated their opinions rather bluntly – "No big ideas," "Stop faking," and "Outdated – in every way."

Still, reading hundreds of reviews was also a positive experience. I found confirmation that DSC3 was one of the better managed warehouses. Whereas a good number of reviewers complained that their managers treated them in a demeaning way, bad mouthed employees, and never helped, I never saw anything of that at DSC3. Also, at DSC3, dealing with huge volumes of work was always a team effort; everybody, including the operations managers, helped.

- 34 -

In June 2020, out of the blue, I sold a paperback copy of my book *BAT SHIT CRAZY Review Requests: Email Humor*.

The sale came as a huge surprise because I had not marketed this particular book in more than two years. Even more baffling was the fact that Amazon's author dashboard stated that I netted only 25 cents from the sale of this paperback book.

25 CENTS?

I quickly did the math.

The book cost $6. Ten percent of $6 are 60 cents and five percent are 30 cents. Which meant that I, the author and creator of the book, earned 4 percent of the sale. And Amazon, the printer, publisher, and distributor of my book, received 96 percent.

Could this be right? I investigated the facts at Amazon's help page "Paperback Pricing > Royalty."

Amazon paid authors 60 percent of the list price if the book was sold at their site but only 40 percent if the book was sold at any other U.S. bookstore. Of these 60 or 40 percent respectively, Amazon deducted the printing costs, in this case $2.15.

40 percent of $6.00 equaled $2.40. Minus $2.15 equaled $0.25 – a quarter.

As soon as I read these facts, I remembered that I read them when I uploaded my book, two years ago. I agreed to these royalties because I wanted "everybody" to be able to buy my book, including "outliers" who by principle did not shop at Amazon.

The only thing I did not know was that seeing the words "Your Royalties – $0.25" would feel so humiliating.

A movie scene came to mind.

It was the opening scene from Mel Brooks' movie *Life Stinks* which shows billionaire Goddard Bolt's Rolls Royce driving around a corner where a few homeless people sleep on the sunny sidewalk. The Rolls drives through a puddle and douses the homeless with the cold, dirty water.

As I stared at the words "Your Royalties – $0.25" I felt like the homeless must have felt.

And so I wondered if I should opt out of Amazon's extended distribution program. Or, maybe, I should investigate if other publishers offered higher royalties?

In 2012, when I published my first book in the United States, choosing Amazon-Createspace was a no-brainer. At the time no other publishing company could print-on-demand and deliver books as quickly as they did. Since I am a loyal person, I never checked out any other print-on-demand publishers.

As I reminisced about the days I was working on releasing my first book, I remembered how happy I felt even while proofreading my book for the nth time. After Florian died, I thought I'd never be able to publish a book again. It was Amazon who helped me make it happen. The truth was that had Amazon not launched a self-publishing service, I would have missed out on some awesome experiences.

Wasn't all this worth losing a dollar every now and then?

If I was honest with myself, being able to write books and scoring a big success here or there kept me balanced all these years. Up to the year my husband died I never had an "uncreative job." Never ever. I used to make movies, design books, write books, create marketing campaigns, and write scripts for commercials.

But in the United States, my excellent education, past work experiences, or being bilingual did not help me to land any of these jobs. In the U.S., I was a person who went to "some university somewhere in Europe," never mind that my alma mater is associated with twenty-one Nobel prize winners.

Never a complainer I did the next best thing and turned my organizational skills into a new career, or better – into a few new careers. And I was okay with it. My top priority was to help my children build their lives. Then, totally unexpectedly, Amazon gave me the opportunity to continue writing books without having to invest large sums of money I did not have. And I loved them for it.

While I did not owe Amazon-Createspace anything, most certainly I appreciated the fact the company's offerings allowed me to do things that made my life richer. Hence, it was childish to feel humiliated by that horrible number "$0.25."

All was good. It was probably that Covid-related stress which ticked me off.

- 35 -

Meanwhile, strange things began happening at DSC3. Though management offered VTO (Voluntary-Time-Off) almost every day, they also hired new people almost every week. To me, this made no sense. If DSC3 already employed more associates than they needed, why were they hiring even more people? I decided to ask Google, just for fun.

Most surprisingly, the search engine offered an answer.

On June 13, 2018, while Amazon's search for their HQ2 was still ongoing, *Gizmodo* published an article by Bryan Menegus titled "On Amazon's Time." The article speculated that Amazon might be hiring more workers than they needed to take advantage of tax incentives which were given based on how many workers Amazon hired and retained.

"Oh my," I sighed because that idea seemed to explain – EVERYTHING! The subpar training, the lack of quality control, the ill-designed stowing racks, management's odd reaction to my complaint about the worn-out scanners, and the fact that nobody seemed to care that DSC3's associates were forced to bend down dozens of times per night to pick up ultralight plastic mailers.

Whereas I wondered why management did not see that these were the reasons why people quit – maybe – Amazon Logistics did not care if people quit. They could always hire more people.

Maybe this was the real reason why Amazon set up their logistics division?

Forget 53-foot billboards. Opening more warehouses gave Amazon the opportunity to employ hundreds of thousands of low-wage workers and get hundreds of millions of dollars in tax incentives.

Plus, at the time I started working at DSC3, delivery stations hired only part-time workers who did not get health insurance through the company. It was only when the Covid-crisis struck that DSC3 began offering opportunities to work 30 hours per week and get that health insurance.

I also remembered Amazon's HQ2 competition. When the company announced their request for proposals, I thought that the search for HQ2 was about transforming a medium-sized American city into a city of the future, similar to what some Asian and Middle Eastern countries were doing.

When Amazon finally announced the winners – New York City and Arlington, Virginia – I was dumbstruck. Why'd they even hold a competition? Certainly, New York City and greater Washington, DC were already "on the map."

Now, one-and-a-half years later, I believed I knew the answer to this question – Amazon's search for HQ2 was a different version of their power hour.

Most likely, Amazon had a short list of contenders even before they released their request for proposal (just like DSC3's management knew who among their stowers stood a chance at winning the power hour). The only thing Amazon could not know was the amount of tax incentives the competing cities would offer (just like DSC3's management could not know who among their stowers was going to work extra hard on a specific day.)

By making their competition public, Amazon gave city and state officials a reason to "try harder."

Still – why did Amazon's executives not see that their power hour was a flawed concept?

Sometimes, people who assess their own numbers don't want to win because they feel that the cost of winning is too high. (For example, DSC3's stowers had no problem relating the "costs in physical pain" to the benefit of potentially winning a $25 gizmo they did not need.)

Since the HQ2-bids were confidential, apparently, New Yorkers did not know that Mayor Bill de Blasio and Governor Andrew Cuomo offered Amazon $1.4 billion of tax credits and $1.1 billion in grants if Amazon built their HQ2 in New York City.

Once the facts were released, many New Yorkers weren't too thrilled. Just as DSC3's stowers questioned their desire to win, New Yorkers wondered about theirs. Rents would be going up and income and racial inequality were going to rise. Plus, transit improvements, new housing, and new schools would have to be funded, but the city would not receive the needed tax revenue from Amazon. So, New Yorkers rebelled against the HQ2-deal and Amazon withdrew their offer.

To me, Amazon's HQ2 story was quite disappointing, and so was Amazon's Covid-response. *Why did this company never want to create the kind of change Americans would still be talking about 100 years from now, especially since the company could afford it easily?*

In selecting a hometown for HQ2 that was not already a huge player like New York City or greater Washington, DC, Amazon could have started to build a city of the future. And, they could have made an impact that would have been reflected in the city's (new) nickname; similar to Boston being Bean Town, Detroit – Motor City, Houston – Space City, Pittsburgh – Steel City, and Rochester – 'The World's Image Centre (in the '80s and 90's).' When I attended high school in Austria, I learned these cities' nicknames, because they stood for American greatness.

Alas, Amazon passed on this kind of opportunity. And, sadly, they also passed on the opportunity to make history by paying a "facemask wearing compensation." In my opinion, it was even worse.

Certainly, Amazon knew that their associates at the delivery centers did not make enough money to feed a family with one or two children because they offered only 24-hour or 30-hour workweeks at these warehouses.

24 hours times $16 ($15 plus $1 night shift differential) is only $384 per week (before taxes) and 30 hours times $16 comes out to $480 per week (before taxes). When the Covid crisis struck, many of the delivery center associates became their families' sole breadwinners. In many cases one parent had to stay home and home-educate the children. Receiving an additional $2 per hour would have put another $48 to $60 per week into these worker's wallets, which would have helped them.

Even more importantly, by paying their warehouse employees a "facemask wearing compensation for as long as the crisis lasted" Amazon would have redefined the role which huge U.S. employers can play in times of crisis.

But instead of becoming a trailblazer, Amazon established a relief fund with $25 million to support their independent delivery drivers and their seasonal employees. The way it looked to me, crisis-affected employees had to beg for money.

Why couldn't the company(ies) who received millions of dollars in tax incentives spread some of the benefits they received?

If they could not come up with this idea on their own, there ought to be a law passed; a law that required that, in times of a national crisis, Fortune 500 companies who received tax incentives were required to give back to the people they employed. Because the tax incentives they received were meant to create good jobs for American citizens and taxpayers. If, during a national crisis, people who were gainfully employed had to resort to seeking assistance, obviously, the employer who got the tax incentives did not meet that goal.

- 36 -

Of course, saving money and time was important to me too, as a widowed mom and as a professional.

However, to me it was never about "How much can I (or we) rake in?" but about "How can we make things better?" I always thought this way because I started my career in the movie industry. In that industry, people who did not value time and money and who didn't ponder making their work the best it could be didn't make it. And, when I worked for my husband's aerial photography company, we were always under pressure because we ran a small business.

After Florian's death, my first huge success came when I began working at that construction company that built projects along the entire east coast. There, I observed that the assistants of the project managers sent complete sets of blueprints to all subcontractors who bid our projects – via Fedex Priority Overnight!

The first time I saw the stacks of Fedex tubes lying on the conference table waiting to get picked up I almost fainted. Having worked for Fedex, I could figure out the shipping costs in my head. So, I came up with the idea to add a plan room to the company's website, which, in 2007, was a revolutionary idea.

Ten days later, the plan room was done. Approved subcontractors got a log-in which enabled them to have the blueprints printed at their preferred printshop, in their hometown.

Some of the smaller subcontractors didn't want to go along; they still worked with typewriters and fax machines. I told them, "Please don't worry about a thing. I'll fax you an instructions sheet which you can take to your printer. The printer will know what to do and twenty minutes later you'll have your blueprints." It worked.

But while my boss only raved that I helped the company save thousands of dollars, I had another reason to be proud of myself – besides saving time and money, my idea helped in cutting CO2 emissions. Our blueprints did not have to get shipped anymore, let alone shipped by airplane.

At DSC3, I was so bored that I thought about these kinds of topics all the time.

Were the white-blue lightweight plastic mailers really the best solution to packing and shipping so many different items? Why didn't we use more of Amazon's recyclable paper padded mailers? They were not slippery, never got blown off the conveyors, could be stowed easier because they were stiffer, and they could be placed in curbside recycle bins.

Amazon said that their white-blue mailers could be recycled but I knew this was not happening in my home state South Carolina.

When I called my city's recycle center to ask if the white-blue mailers could be placed in the recycle roll carts or had to be dropped off at one of the city's collection sites, the person who answered the phone only laughed and said, "Hon, them Amazon envelopes aren't recycled in all of South Carolina. They jam up our machines. If you put them into the roll cart for recyclables, we have to throw them in the trash. Please don't do that that because it's only more work for us."

And so, I kept hating the white-blue mailers. I also hoped that eventually, Amazon would use more recyclable paper padded mailers.

It never happened. Instead, after the Covid crisis began, we received disproportionally more white-blue mailers. In fact, we received so many jiffies that my "bookend-stowing tip" became obsolete.

There was no telling why this was happening. Did Amazon pack items which previously were shipped in boxes into plastic mailers? Or, did Amazon's customers order more small items which they used to buy at brick-and-mortar stores before Covid?

One thing was certain – this time I was not going to volunteer my idea to speed up stowing the vast amounts of jiffies. Because it made no sense.

Obviously, every new method had to be tested. To figure out if this one could save a significant amount of time, DSC3 would have to run at least two weeks of experiments – allowing one excellent stower and one mediocre stower to work with the new method while a control group of an excellent stower and a mediocre stower worked with the traditional method – in designated aisles where no other stowers could interfere.

But these were two things DSC3 never did. They required all stowers to work in many aisles so the good stowers made up for the shortcomings of others. Plus, DSC3 never ran any experiments.

It was my biggest disappointment about working at DSC3. I did not mind the hard work or the ridiculous target rates. Having lived through rough times, I was used to working insanely hard. But I thought that I'd be working for an organization who lived up to what they said about themselves. Instead, it appeared that Amazon Logistics hoped all their people would adopt "Boxer's" work habits, Boxer from *Animal Farm*.

Then, one early morning, as I was patrolling my cluster at the end of my shift, I saw a white-blue mailer lying on the floor between two stowing shelves. Of course, I went to pick it up and stow it into the correct bag.

It was a light jiffy that contained a soft, medium-sized item. Much to my surprise, as I lifted the mailer, its content fell out. This never happened before. I inspected the mailer. It was busted open on one side.

Then, I stared at the item on the floor. I could hardly believe my eyes.

"The item" was a multi-pack of a commonly used household item. I myself purchased these things for under five bucks at my supermarket. Even gas stations carried them.

Why would anybody order just one multi-pack of this widely available product at Amazon?

The only answer I could come up with was that the customer forgot to buy the item when they went grocery shopping and, to avoid having to go back and potentially expose themselves to more Covid dangers, they ordered the forgotten item at Amazon.

I put the product back into its jiffy, scanned it, and placed it in the section where the problem solvers would find it. They would tape it up again.

"These darn jiffies," I thought and then – stopped dead in my tracks. An idea shot through my mind.

I turned around and stared at the bags on the shelves.

Oh, so many jiffies!

How many of them were filled with benign items, like the one that fell out of the busted mailer?

If it was true that shipping one package cost Amazon between $2 and $3, there was no way Amazon made a profit on that sale. Maybe they did not even cut even on this purchase.

In July 2020 Amazon shipped more than 100 million items per week. Who knew how many benign, cheap items were among these purchases?

Was this the reason why Amazon began shipping so many products in white-blue jiffies? Because the plastic jiffies were cheaper to produce than Amazon's recyclable paper-padded mailers?

On Change.org, 527,409 consumers signed a petition: "Ask Amazon to reduce the amount of plastic used for packing" and 738,198 consumers signed a petition: "Get Amazon to Offer Plastic-Free Packaging Options."

If Amazon really believed that their jiffies could be recycled successfully, why didn't they try to "obsess" over these online petitioners' wishes and start a recycling business?

They already dabbled in so many different industries – from selling books, over selling "everything" including groceries, to creating autonomous vehicles for self-driving transport services and much more.

In fact, to speed up things, Amazon could simply buy a recycle business and improve on that business' operations, like they did with so many other types of businesses. Most likely, American consumers would prefer that business concept over Amazon wiping out other retail stores.

- 37 -

Though most of DSC3's workers suffered from foot pain, I never did. I was and am an enthusiastic hiker. In the weeks before I started working at DSC3 I trained for the Paris Mountain 25K race, speed walking up and down that mountain at least five times per week. At work, I only worried about hurting my back.

Alas, in June 2020, I started to develop calluses on my fingers. I found this puzzling until I realized that the constant handwashing and using alcohol-based hand-sanitizers did not go well with wearing box-handling gloves. The gloves were "rubbing" on my dry hands six hours per night. I tried to deal with the problem by using my grandma's old trick of applying moisturizer and sleeping with gloves on.

Then, in early August 2020, not quite a year since I started working at DSC3, pain set in. At first, it was not even real pain but my hand grip strength was gone. I could not open sealed jars anymore, which was a bit of an issue because I love snacking on crisp kosher dill pickles. I also had trouble pulling apart cereal box liners and the kind of plastic bags which are used to package salads.

It was a strange feeling – one of powerlessness. Since I was a teenager, I was the "handy kid" among my parents' four children, the one who painted walls, laid floors, and installed ceiling fans as a hobby. But all of a sudden, I could not open a cereal box liner.

Shortly thereafter real pain set in, a type of pain I never knew existed.

At least three out of five workdays, I experienced a stabbing pain in my lateral fingernail grooves. On some days, the pain was so bad that I tossed and turned for a good hour before I fell asleep – after working like a mule for six hours. At first, I thought I might have a nail fungus from wearing the same work gloves for too long, but that was not the case.

I was suffering from repetitive motion disorder, which most often affects hands or arms. My pain stemmed from having to "clasp with my fingers" tens of thousands of slippery jiffies. Not holding jiffies but clasping them, because the darn things are slippery.

The best way to treat repetitive motion disorder is to reduce or stop the motion that causes the symptom. The next best way is to take painkillers and rest the affected body part as much as possible, which was the option I chose. And, when my hands hurt too much, I took a day off from work, or booked a few hours of PTO (Personal Time Off).

Of course, I could have requested to perform a different task at DSC3, but I did not want to do that. Having tried out other jobs I knew I was doing the only job at which I could excel for months in a row.

The other position I liked was "inductor." Inductors had to scan between 1,200 and 1,500 packages per hour and also apply the stickers which listed the codes of the bags. I did well in this position as long as I was asked to induct jiffies and smaller packages. Eventually, one of the assistant managers had the not-so-great idea that I was performing so well that I should induct big boxes. That's when things went downhill within two days. After all, I was a person with gray hair, 58 years old.

Since the conveyor was about three feet high, I had to lift the heavy barcode scanner about five feet high so I could scan the barcode on top of the big boxes and apply the stickers, every 3 to 4 seconds – for six hours. There was no opportunity to take a two or three second break because the conveyor kept delivering boxes. So, on day 2 of having to induct big boxes, I threatened that I'd quit if they put me on this job one more time.

I also diverted packages a few times. "Diverter" was a cool name for a very annoying job. The diverters had to pull or push packages and big boxes from one conveyor to another or push or pull the items to either to the right or the left side of a conveyor.

Lastly, there was the position of "picker," which I hated the most. Basically, the pickers lifted packages off a conveyor and placed them on the baker's racks, which on a regular day in 2019 was not a bad job but, during Peak and once the Covid crisis started, it was.

During the first six months of the Covid-crisis, people ordered literally "everything" – from all things that go in a conference room, including the furniture, to shipments of enough high-end water to cross the Sahara – on a camel.

Too many of these boxes weighed 40 pounds and up, which was why I worried about getting hurt accidentally. When the big boxes came down the conveyor it was impossible to tell if the box was a big and light box or a big and heavy box. Therefore, the pickers could only guess the boxes' weights before they pulled them off the conveyor.

The stowers did not have that problem. They could check the box's label which listed its weight. Of course, doing that cost valuable time but I knew I could make it up by trying to stow the jiffies faster, which was probably the reason why, after a year of doing precisely that I developed a repetitive motion disorder.

For the next few weeks I did almost nothing at home; I needed to rest my hands as much as possible.

On the positive side, DSC3 got a new manager who was not an Amazon-man. Pretty soon, I got a chance to bring up the topic of the sluggish scanners for the fourth time. I showed him my stats to illustrate how getting new scanners would improve the stowers' and DSC3's performance rates. He acted upon my suggestion. Though he did not acquire new scanners, at least, he had many of the old scanners repaired.

This made me hopeful. Maybe I finally had a boss who realized that the fact that I, though not a yes-girl, helped the warehouse perform better and avoid potential problems?

I also noticed other positive changes – DSC3 received fewer dented boxes. Maybe Amazon Logistics chose a different cardboard for their boxes or maybe the boxes got handled differently at the fulfillment centers?

Soon thereafter, when a small group of us VTOed, I also saw that the assistant manager checked her laptop after every scan and that she double-scanned two associates' badges "because the first scan didn't register."

Even more remarkably, on Youtube I saw a video of a new delivery station where they used bakers' racks instead of shelves to hold the bags. The racks held only three rows of bags. Apparently, somebody at Amazon Logistics figured out that the average American woman is only 5 foot 4 tall.

Maybe, change was in the air?

- 38 -

Indeed, pretty soon something new came up, but it was not a change I was looking for.

Though I did not really market any of my books since the Covid crisis began, I regularly checked if somebody posted a review for one of them. Then, one day, as I searched for my name in Amazon's store, three books of competitors popped up – in the top position of the page, ahead of my books. There was a tiny remark on the side – "Sponsored." Next to the word "Sponsored" was a feedback button asking if the ad was "appropriate" and "how appropriate" it was.

"NOT AT ALL," I yelled at my monitor. "Showing a person who is looking for books penned by Gisela Hausmann books penned by Jane Doe is not appropriate under any circumstances."

I was furious.

How many thousands of hours did I spend building my brand?

Now Amazon used my work and the traffic I generated to sell their ads?

I drove traffic to them and in return they drove my traffic to a different author?

And what the dickens happened to their guiding principle of customer obsession?

Did they consider that people who searched for my books actually wanted to see my books and not somebody else's?

I searched for Maya Angelou's books. Not surprisingly, Amazon's search results showed me books from another poet at the top of the page.

Thank God, I decided not to promote my books during the pandemic. At least I did not pay anybody for creating interest in my books which Amazon could use to show my fans my competitors' books.

A thought popped up in my mind – What about cell phones searches? Cell phone screens were much smaller than my nice, big monitor.

I decided to look for another famous author – Oprah Winfrey, beloved talk show host and advisor on self-improvement, mindfulness, and spirituality. Oprah even had her own book club and she could sell millions of books by just mentioning a title.

But, like I feared, I had to scroll on my cellphone to actually see her books. And the same was true when I searched for "Oprah's book club."

This was worse than ridiculous. What happened to Amazon's credo that they were obsessed with giving their customers what they wanted? Nobody who was looking for Oprah's books wanted to see these other books *before* they got to see Oprah's books.

In contrast to the $0.25-issue this new situation could not be ignored. Because not only did it affect every book I published in the past, it also affected everything I'd do in the future.

I called my trusted friend in Vienna.

He listened and then said, "So, basically Amazon is doing the same thing as Google."

"Yep," I said. "Same thing, but HUGE difference. Google is a search engine and Amazon is an ecommerce store. Since Google is a search engine, they need to show ads to make money. In contrast, ecommerce sites are shopping venues. Amazon gets their share off all purchases. Of course, there is nothing wrong with showing ads, but the ads should be below the item the customer really wants to see."

"Right," my friend said. "I didn't even think this through."

"One sec," I went on. "Let me look for a product instead of a book. How about Campbell's Tomato Soup?"

This time, I did not set Amazon's pulldown menu to 'Grocery & Gourmet Food' but to 'All Products.' I wanted to see if Amazon's search engine would pull up art prints of Andy Warhol's famous painting.

Seeing the search results, I almost fell off my chair. "You are not going to believe this," I said. "Guess what Amazon is showing me."

"I have no idea."

"Two kinds of beef broths and one chicken soup."

"That's just plain stupid," my friend replied. "I am a vegetarian. Though tomato soup is not my favorite, I'd eat it if I had to. But I would never eat beef broth or chicken soup."

"Oh, ghee, I did not even think about the fact that you are a vegetarian." I kept scrolling through Amazon's search results. Amazon showed me a few different kinds of tomato soups, plus wedding soup, cream of mushrooms, and also my favorite – lentil soup – on page 1. There were more offerings of Campbell's tomato soups on pages 2,3,4, and 5 and other soups but not one art print featuring Andy Warhol's painting.

This was extremely odd because Amazon sells wall art, t-shirts, tote bags, candles, coffee mugs, and phone cases which feature Andy Warhol's painting "Campbell's tomato soup can."

"And?" my friend asked. "What do you think?"

"Well, like you pointed out, it's lousy customer service. No vegetarian would think that Amazon is obsessed with making them smile if Amazon's search results show them beef broth ahead of tomato soup."

I was looking for a way to illustrate what I wanted to say.

"Remember that I told you that, in Wilmington, I used to live in walking distance of three Harris Teeter supermarkets? I shopped there a lot. If, at a Harris Teeter supermarket, a customer asks where they can find a specific product, the clerk does not reply, "Soups are in aisle 7." The clerk walks the customer to the product. And, once clerk and customer arrive in the correct section, the clerk does not say, 'There are the soups' but points at the specific soup you were looking for. THAT is exceptional customer service! One feels like they are in the forties when bellhops escorted people to their hotel rooms."

"Oh wow," my friend said. "They used to do that at Meindl's in downtown Vienna. But I don't shop there anymore since I moved to the 'burbs' like you Americans say. So, what are you going to do?"

"I don't know yet. It seems like a stupid idea to publish more books on Amazon. A – Why should I work off my butt so they can use my work to show my fans books from other authors? And – B – if Amazon thinks that it is a good idea to show customers sponsored ads ahead of the products they want to see, who knows what idea the company might come up with next?"

"Yeah, this is crazy. But doesn't Amazon worry that authors leave?"

"Well, I guess they think they can do anything they like. After all, Amazon owns 70 percent of the ebook market. One of my acquaintances, an author who is also a lawyer publishes all her books with everybody but Amazon. And just recently I read that a huge U.S. bookstore by the name of Powell, which is located somewhere in the Northwest, won't sell on Amazon anymore."

"Just like my Birkenstocks," my friend mused. "But that's because people sold counterfeits on Amazon. Now I buy my sandals at the Birkenstock store at the Donauzentrum. Oh, and my running shoes, my Nikes... They quit selling on Amazon too."

"Yep, I know."

"So, will you quit selling on Amazon?"

"I don't know yet. I guess quitting means that I'd have to pull all my already published books off Amazon. That is a problem, a huge problem. Combined, my books have more than 500 reviews on Amazon. They own these reviews because all these years I drove all traffic to them."

I sighed.

"You know what I hate the most about all of this? In my book about Facebook for authors, I wrote, 'Don't put all your eggs in one basket. If you collect all your contacts on Facebook, eventually you are going to have to pay for ads so your contacts get to see your postings.'

That's how smart I was! Now I am in the same boat, only the vessel's name is Amazon. Almost all of my reviews are on their site. And, apparently, Amazon wants me to buy ads so they will show my books to my fans.

Of course, I thought they were on my side. Because they are my publisher. They make money off my book sales. Alas, it turns out even Facebook is nicer. At least, they show me one of my friends' postings before they show me their first ad."

My friend giggled. "You found something positive about Facebook? I think I need a drink."

"Well, it's a fact that these online giants evaluate their data and change their ways of running their sites according to what's best for them. However, what Amazon did here is a horrible change. It's not good for their vendors and not good for their customers."

- 39 -

As summer turned into fall, I was curious to see if I would ever get a pay raise. August 30, the anniversary of my hire date, came and went but my hourly wage was still $15 plus $1 night shift differential; the same as the associates' who got hired the previous week.

Given the turnover rate of Amazon Logistics' workers, I thought that Amazon might be eager to demonstrate that they valued the work of well-performing employees like me, but, apparently, their perspective was entirely different.

At the beginning of October 2020, Amazon associates began chatting about upcoming pay raises on one of the social media platforms where Amazon warehouse employees discussed work-related topics.

Somebody said that they heard that Amazon was going to raise our hourly wages to a minimum of $17 or $18 because the company wanted to undermine unionization efforts. Other group members thought Amazon was only going to raise the wages at the warehouses where they had a hard time filling positions. Again others predicted that Amazon would not raise the hourly pay before Peak season was over and all seasonal workers were laid off. Clearly, everybody who commented on the topic had a good working knowledge of how American capitalism works.

About three weeks later, on October 25, all my friends and acquaintances at DSC3 got a pay raise of 30 cents per hour, including "White Badges" (temporary associates) who worked at DSC3 for only two weeks.

And I? – I got a pay raise of 55 cents per hour, a quarter more than the others.

But while I thought that maybe my efforts to excel had been noticed my friends were quick to point out that most likely I received a higher pay-raise because I worked 30 hours per week, whereas all of them worked only 24 hours per week. Still, nobody was jealous because my extra 25 cents per hour added up to only $7.50 – per week.

Not a number to write home about.

Another four weeks later, on November 21, my first-year anniversary of becoming a regular part-time employee (a "Blue Badge"), I received another pay raise of 25 cents, in other words – an additional $7.50 per week. Considering that I worked at twice the speed of about 20 percent of DSC3's stowers I thought that raise was rather shabby.

Still, what shocked me the most was the fact that – apparently – my first eleven weeks at DSC3, when I worked as a temporary employee (a "White Badge"), did not get counted toward my first year of employment. The way things looked, from August 30, 2019 to November 21, 2019 I was a package-handling ghost.

I had never heard of anything like this. While the concept that an employer wanted to evaluate a new hire's performance before promoting them to a regular position made a lot of sense, mathematically speaking, it made no sense that my first 11 weeks at DSC3 were not part of my first 52 weeks at DSC3.

There are few things in life which I detest more than maneuvers like this. Obviously, anybody who tried to pull off a trick most fourth graders could figure out operated on the assumption that most everybody around them was stupid. I did not want to believe that the second most valuable company in the world would do a thing like that.

Attempting to recollect how this conversion from "White Badge" to "Blue Badge" went down, I remembered that I had to fill out a second application to do the same job I did during the preceding eleven weeks. And that I received quite a bit of correspondence regarding this matter.

I opened my Amazon-Job email folder. The emails relating to my conversion said that Amazon would "communicate" the date of my New Hire Orientation "in the near future" and what I needed to do "prior to my first day on-site."

What new hire? What orientation? And, what first day on-site? At the time, I was working at DSC3, four nights per week.

Was this outlandish move an example of Amazon's "Day 1"-thinking? – Pushing out my hire date by 12 weeks so they would not have to pay me 12 times $7.50, or $90 respectively?

They could not be that cheap, or could they?

As I looked through more emails, one of them caught my eye. It was a group email that informed DSC3's associates that power had been restored at the warehouse after Tropical Storm Zeta caused 80,000 power outages in the region, including at the warehouse.

Typically, group emails have handles that define the group the email is addressed to, such as To:sales@company or To:hr@company.

The group email address of DSC3's associates was, "To:Nobody@company."

In my birth country Austria, we called that a Freudian slip.

- 40 -

By mid-November things got really stressful. First, DSC3 reported noticeably more Covid cases. Of course, this was not Amazon's fault, and everybody knew it. For weeks, Dr. Anthony Fauci warned that the winter months would be the most difficult in the public health history of the United States. Obviously, since the winter weather forced Americans indoors, the virus was going to spread faster.

I expected that Amazon would step up their efforts to ensure that all associates obeyed all safety measures. After all, it was not only winter season but also Peak season.

Still, I did not notice any additional efforts other than the company giving their associates the opportunity to get Covid-tested for free while also getting paid the same money as if they were working.

As the number of cases was rising, one of my acquaintances caught the virus, which freaked me out. Since this person was an all-around friendly human who had many friends, I wondered if this person might have passed on the virus to others at DSC3. After that happened, even socializing in the parking lot felt like a dangerous activity.

No one who was not working at one of the warehouses will ever know what it was really like – processing thousands of shipments while working in silence like a Trappist monk. I even prayed a lot, for example, "Dear Lord, don't let there be another dozen packages weighing more than 40 pounds in the next aisle."

Most of my colleagues seemed to have similar thoughts. During every break, about half of DSC3's crew "fled" outside to spend their breaktime in the safety of their cars. Thank God, the weather cooperated. During all of November, temperatures dipped below freezing only twice.

Then, on November 23, *VICE's* magazine *'Motherboard'* broke the news that Amazon hired Pinkerton, a private security contractor, to spy on their warehouse workers. This news did not surprise me.

A couple of weeks earlier, Amazon set up "distance assistants" in DSC3's breakroom and in the stand-up area. Like typical CCTV security systems, they recorded all activities and displayed the images on enormous monitors. As an improvement to typical CCTV security systems, the monitors showed each person surrounded with a green circle which turned red if two persons walked or stood within 6-feet of each other.

On paper or in a short video, the system looked like a clever invention. However, in real life, it did not help.

Because the systems did not emit any auditory signals, they were only useful if people watched the monitor while walking (like robots) to their assigned stations. However, if associates behaved like humans and stopped to chat with a friend, the security system was useless. Obviously, people who communicated with each other looked at each other's faces, not at the monitors. Also, people who stood to the side of the monitors could not see the images at all.

Therefore, the most logical explanation seemed to be that the "distance assistants" recorded who was talking with whom and for how long.

I also knew that Amazon had been "spying on" and "infiltrating" online platforms in the past. In 2015, the technology news website *Geekwire* revealed, "After undercover sting, Amazon files suit against 1,000 Fiverr users over fake product reviews" (by Jacob Demmitt).

That spying mission had a clear purpose – to purge Amazon's review platform of fake reviews and to make it clear that Amazon was not going to tolerate this kind of illegal activities. Even better, as a side benefit, Amazon's 2015 sting operation benefitted their honest business partners – indie authors and vendors who did not cheat.

In contrast, spying on workers who might want to form a union was not cool. And it did not have any side benefits. However, what annoyed me the most was that – apparently – Amazon went about this activity in a remarkably uncreative way. The way I saw it, they did not demonstrate "Day 1"-thinking or even "Day 2"-thinking but "Day 0"-thinking, a kind of thinking that was popular at the turn of the 1900s.

In my opinion, true "Day 1"-thinkers would have looked at the issue from a totally different perspective. They would have said, "Though the Covid-crisis causes enormous strain for our workers we (really) don't want to pay them more money. So – how can we show good will? What can we do for them to make their lives better?"

It would not have taken Sherlock Holmes (or Pinkerton consultants) to solve this riddle. The information was publicly accessible on social media platforms, the very platforms where, allegedly, Pinkerton spied on Amazon's workers.

There, Amazon's associates vented about how much they hated handling the almost insane number of shipments of dog food, cat litter, and packs of 24 bottles of high-end waters.

All the items had two things in common: A – they weighed more than 40 pounds and – B – because of the Covid-crisis Amazon sold them like hot cakes. As a result, during the summer of 2020, which was the Northern Hemisphere's hottest meteorological summer, Amazon's associates moved more super-heavy packages than ever inside hot warehouses, while also having to wear facemasks. And, since Amazon phased out their hazard pay before the summer season began, Amazon's associates had to do the heavy lifting without receiving any additional compensation.

THIS could have been avoided.

All Amazon needed to do was to announce to the public, "In order to improve the working conditions of our essential workers who have to wear facemasks, we will not sell and ship packages of dog food, cat litter, and packs of high-end waters weighing more than 30 pounds." (Obviously, anybody who needed larger quantities could always order multiple packages.)

If Amazon would have taken this course of action their associates and delivery drivers would have rejoiced, and Amazon Logistics would have had a much easier time "selling" the concept that they "responded to their workers' needs."

How come Amazon's leadership could not figure this out? And why did Pinkerton not suggest such an idea? (Even children as young as 4 know how to barter.)

Did Amazon believe that their customers would say, "Hell no, we insist that your people slave in hot warehouses while also having to wear facemasks"?

Quite the opposite was true. After Amazon began airing their "Thank-you, Heroes"-commercials Amazon's customers cried out loud, on social media platforms. "Give them better hazard pay if they mean so much to you", "They deserve hazard pay. They are risking their lives", and "Hey, Amazon how about putting your money where your mouth is?"

But – apparently – the "most customer orientated company in the world" did not want to "delight" their customers.

And so it happened that by end of November 2020 Amazon's warehouse workers had handled 127.1 million bags of pet food and who-knows-how-many boxes of cat litter and packs of 24 high-end waters.

And Amazon gave their associates a "Thank-you"-t-shirt and a "Thank-You"-button.

Since I grew up in Europe which has different employment laws, I did not have an opinion about unions and unionization efforts for the longest time. However, once the Pinkerton story broke, things became pretty clear.

If, even with the help of Pinkerton, Amazon could not figure out what they could do to make their workers happier during the Covid crisis, clearly a union was needed. Somebody needed to spell out the solutions Amazon and Pinkerton could not come up with.

Apparently, they did not understand that each of these 127.1 million bags of pet food had to be moved by at least nine different associates (3 at the fulfillment centers, 5 at the delivery centers, plus a delivery driver) in under twelve seconds while also having to wear a facemask, during an extremely hot summer.

- 41 -

Still – the Pinkerton story was only half the news. Also, on November 23, *the Washington Post* reported that the workers at Amazon's warehouse in Bessemer, Alabama, BHM1, filed for a union election through the National Labor Relations Board.

But, though – apparently – American capitalist corporations perceive efforts to unionize as the worst threat to running their businesses, I did not see any efforts to address this "extraordinary threat" in an extraordinary way.

2020 was a year of social activism and huge economic troubles fueled by the pandemic. Most Americans experienced an enormous amount of stress. People were looking for signs of hope and possibility.

Therefore, for Jeff Bezos, the timing could not have been better to portray himself as a leader who cared.

Peak season was on.

The Covid-virus was causing havoc.

The state of affairs was somewhat war-like.

Hence, if I were Jeff Bezos, I would have visited at least a dozen selected warehouses, thanked the workers in person, reminded everybody to do everything they could to protect themselves and their coworkers, and – most importantly – asked them for suggestions to get through Peak season as best as possible.

Probably, just a few such visits would have impressed many warehouse workers and, for sure, they would have earned Jeff Bezos glowing media coverage.

All it would have taken was a bit of creativity and three days of work. For example, at a warehouse like DSC3, Mr. Bezos could have safely entered through the bay doors in the back of the warehouse and then gotten on a scissor lift which could have elevated him high enough so all employees could see him from their usual workstations.

It could have been epic. Spartan environments like warehouses make phenomenal backdrops.

Standing on a scissor lift, Jeff Bezos could have held a great speech which he could have concluded by announcing that every warehouse worker would receive an additional Christmas bonus – a free Prime membership, for as long as they worked at Amazon, which would have been fitting. After all, it was them who moved the goods. (This too, was nothing new. When I worked for Fedex I received an employee discount of minus 80 percent. At the time, I shipped all my family letters to Europe via Fedex Express.)

"Bezos meets with Amazonians and gives Prime memberships on top of Christmas bonuses" would have trended on Twitter.

But, he missed it.

Amazon missed it.

Were there any "Day 1"-thinkers at Amazon?

Of course, there was also the "cheap option" to record a few short video messages which could be aired on a weekly basis throughout Peak season. Doing that would have occupied Mr. Bezos no longer than one or two hours.

Alas, Amazon did what they always did. Instead of coming up with a creative image campaign they promised warehouse employees who worked from December 1st to December 31st a Peak Season bonus. At least, it was higher than the previous year. $300 for full-time workers and $150 for part-time workers.

Online chatter seemed to suggest that the bonuses were paid out on January 29, 2021.

- 42 -

Looking back, I believe I kept hoping that, eventually, I would get to see one or more remarkable problem-solving approaches. Because of that, I never made plans when I was going to quit this job. But, after a year of waiting, my patience wore thin.

With the start of Peak season, I was one of the popular associates again. Every day, between 3:30 and 4:00 a.m., one of the managers stopped by to whine at me, "Can't you stay a little longer today?" They needed people who handled the volume of work which the insufficiently trained people could not process.

But I did not want to do overtime. Since many of the associates did not do their work the way it was supposed to be done, people who "stayed a little longer" had to close and lift dozens of bags weighing more than 40 pounds, so they could stow the remaining packages.

Doing this at 5:00 o'clock in the morning, after working six hours at maximum speed, increased the chances of suffering an injury. I did not want to risk wrecking my lower back and my hands for a measly $16.80 per hour, especially since management ignored every suggestion to optimize the work process.

Plus, there were other annoyances. Though the new manager had the finger scanners fixed, some of them did not properly synch with the smartphones, 100 percent of the time. To avoid having to work with one of these units, I arrived fifteen minutes early at work, almost every night.

Then, in the first week of December, I noticed a new problem – the cleaning staff began taking short-cuts. Naturally, Peak season wore on them too. Every night, DSC3's regular crew plus the seasonal associates plus the VET-shift (Voluntary Extra Time) fixed foods in the many microwave ovens, used the bathrooms, and filled the trash cans to the brim.

This may have been the reason why the cleaning crew came up with an idea to reduce their workload. At the end of their shift, they parked a janitor cart in the doorway of one of the two sections of the ladies' room. Most likely, they wanted to hinder associates from using this section of the ladies' room, so this space did not have to be cleaned again before DSC3's morning shift arrived.

Of course, in doing that the cleaning crew violated Amazon's Covid-safety protocol. Every bathroom was supposed be open, so all associates had the opportunity to wash their hands with soap and warm water as recommended by the CDC (Centers for Disease Control and Prevention).

When I noticed the janitor cart standing in the doorway for the first time, I thought that this happened by accident. I assumed that the cleaning lady had been called away before she could finish her work. But the next day, it happened again, and on the day after that too. For this reason, all women had to use the other section of the ladies' room, which was a problem because many women took off their facemasks in the bathroom.

Considering that this was Covid-days I was not going to touch the cart. I did not know if the carts were used to transport hazardous items, plus, I did not have protective gloves but only porous, breathable box handling gloves.

So, on the third day, I went back to the warehouse, searched for the manager on duty and reported the problem. She agreed with me that the bathroom situation was unacceptable and told me that she would speak with the cleaning crew. And I went home.

As I got up the next morning, I thought that I needed to do more to address this safety issue. For all that mattered, coworkers might have already gotten infected if one or more had to share the relatively small bathroom with an asymptomatic carrier of the virus. So, I sent an email to DSC3's local HR-representative telling him too about the problem. I also included the link to an article from PBS's website, "Public bathrooms carry coronavirus risks. Here's how to be careful" by William Petri, a professor of medicine at the University of Virginia.

Most surprisingly, the HR-representative who never replied to any of my emails in less than 24 hours, responded immediately, stating that he would address the issue right away.

That evening, I could not make it to work fifteen minutes early. Hence, by the time I arrived I could not choose one of the best scanners; there were only a handful of scanners left. The scanner I selected turned out being one of the rather sluggish units. So, to keep up my rate, I exchanged scanners during my lunch break.

Unfortunately, after working with this second scanner for a good forty-five minutes the scanner began to lose connection to the phone intermittently. So I had to take the last package out of the bag, put the package aside, reset the phone, and scan and stow the package again.

Having to do all of this was even more unpleasant if a package had to be stowed into a bag in the bottom row. In that case I needed to get up from the floor, reset the scanner and get down again to scan and stow the package. Basically, I had to do two squats every two to three minutes, after 2:00 o'clock in the morning.

So, I tried to exchange the second scanner but there weren't any left in the bin, a clear indicator that some of my colleagues experienced problems too. But I was not a quitter so I finished working the third work session.

Sore to the point that I could barely stand upright, I went to the manager, explained what was wrong with the scanner and asked her to "really do something" about these problems, for example – acquiring more scanners and more phones. Then, I ended my complaint by saying, "It is kind of hard to understand why the company of the richest man in the world cannot provide new equipment, especially when we are handling Peak volume."

She listened and her face broke into a sympathetic grimace. Then she said in a calm and composed way, "Unfortunately, there is not much I can do about that." It was probably true, but it was not the answer I wanted to hear. I still kept it together and limped to the bathroom to wash my hands.

Naturally, I was in so much pain that I forgot about the janitor cart. But – there it was, again blocking the entrance to one section of the ladies' room.

I stared at the cart and knew – this was it.

I was done with working for Amazon.

It did not matter what I thought about the company in the past. In the last 468 days I could not detect any "Day 1"-thinking. All there was were talking points.

And leadership principles on the lunchroom's walls.

I turned to the exit and did not look back.

- Epilogue -

August 9, 2021

It's been 100 days since I released "Inside Amazon." Big things have happened since then.

On July 1, 2021, Amazon announced two new leadership principles: "Strive to be Earth's Best Employer" and "Success and Scale Bring Broad Responsibility." The company wants to do better for their customers, their employees, their partners, and even – the world at large.

Especially the first of the two goals seems rather lofty for a company whose working conditions have been discussed in the news for more than two decades. Already in 1999, when Amazon was *just*

"Earth's biggest bookstore," the *Washington Post* published an article, "Service Workers Without a Smile At Amazon.com." Thousands of other stories followed.

However, Amazon is not the only company with problems. According to a Microsoft study from June 2021, 41 percent of workers – worldwide – are considering quitting their jobs. And, according to a survey by Monster.com, also conducted in June 2021, 95 percent of U.S. workers were contemplating leaving their jobs. Most of them cite burnout and lack of growth opportunities as their reason.

Naturally, I don't know if Amazon can achieve their lofty goal or if their efforts will stall. Still, I have more trust in them setting new standards than I have in U.S. politicians. A lot of them seem to only play to the media.

I sent this book to a few of the politicians who constantly criticize Amazon for their working conditions. Not one of them even acknowledged the receipt of the book though they have staff for doing that. Hence, one must ask themselves, are they really interested in the working conditions at Amazon, or do they prefer to rant on TV and on social media platforms?

Be this as it may, certainly, Amazon has a record of pursuing their ambitions with breathtaking vigor and the company is not afraid to change the status quo.

In creating and establishing the customer review, Amazon created a new standard for marketing, selling, and buying literally anything, including vegetables. The company also advanced self-publishing and made two-to-three-day purchase-to-delivery the norm. In the same 25 years, during which U.S. politicians could not even manage to raise the federal minimum wage even once, Amazon changed entire industries, in less than a decade.

That is why I see hope.

While I don't know if Amazon will really strive to be "Earth's Best Employer" I am 100 percent certain that ***if*** they do, they will create a situation that forces other companies to jump on the bandwagon. People who are looking for change should pay attention.

THANK YOU for reading my story.

Please post a review. Readers worldwide (and I) would love to read your thoughts, especially if you are or have been an Amazon employee, an indie author or vendor, or a consumer who is concerned about the environment.

A big thank-you also to my co-workers at DSC3 who helped me in keeping up my spirits, especially the three ladies who always helped me. (*You know who you are*.)

Last but not least, a huge thank-you to my family and friends who support me in all my efforts.

Gisela Hausmann

Bibliography

This bibliography is not complete by any measure; it is merely supposed to prove that I am not disclosing "proprietary information." The list is sorted by topics. It does not feature comments from social media platforms.

AMAZON PUBLISHING PLATFORM

"In conversation with Jeff Bezos: CEO of the internet" (*WIRED*/Steven Levy)

https://www.wired.co.uk/article/ceo-of-the-internet

"Revealed: How one Amazon Kindle scam made millions of dollars" (*ZDNet Zero Day*/ Zack Whittaker)

https://www.zdnet.com/article/exclusive-inside-a-million-dollar-amazon-kindle-catfishing-scam/

"Amazon targets abuse of Kindle e-book platform to increase reviews, royalties" (*Seattle Times*/Matt Day)

https://www.seattletimes.com/business/amazon/amazon-targets-abuse-of-kindle-e-book-platform-to-increase-reviews-royalties

"From Amazon, a Change That Hurts Authors" (*New York Times*/Douglas Preston)

https://www.nytimes.com/2017/10/12/opinion/book-publishing-amazon-sales.html

"Amazon has laid out exactly how to game its self-publishing platform" (*Quartz*/Thu-Huong Ha)

https://qz.com/1077996/self-publishing-on-amazon-amzn-how-an-author-can-hack-a-books-success-sales-and-royalties/

"Amazon Won Arbitration That Addresses The Six-Figure 'Book Stuffing' Kindle Scam" (*Forbes*/Adam Rowe)

https://www.forbes.com/sites/adamrowe1/2018/04/07/amazon-has-filed-suit-to-stop-the-six-figure-book-stuffing-kindle-scam/

"Kindle Unlimited Book Stuffing Scam Earns Millions and Amazon Isn't Stopping It" (*Inc.com*/Minda Zetlin)

https://www.inc.com/minda-zetlin/amazon-book-stuffing-authors-scam-chance-carter-romance-kindle-unlimited.html

"Amazon self-published authors: Our books were banned for no reason" (*Yahoo*/JP Mangalindan)

https://finance.yahoo.com/news/amazon-self-published-authors-books-banned-no-reason-134606120.html

"Plagiarism, 'book-stuffing', clickfarms ... the rotten side of self-publishing" (*The Guardian*/Alison Flood)

https://www.theguardian.com/books/2019/mar/28/plagiarism-book-stuffing-clickfarms-the-rotten-side-of-self-publishing

*

DELIVERY STATIONS

Amazon Delivery Station - KMTV 3 News Now

https://youtu.be/uo7S7rr_IgU

Amazon Delivery Station - FOX 8 News Cleveland

https://youtu.be/fY4vfCXtApM

Amazon Delivery Center - KFOR Oklahoma

https://youtu.be/bx72jjo5jQI

Conveyors at Delivery Station. This Amazon stock picture makes it appear as if working along a conveyor is an easy task. In reality, "piles of items" came down the conveyor, especially during Peak season and Covid days. From March 15 to December 9, 2020 I never saw any conveyor at DSC3 look "that empty," apart from the beginning and the end of the shift.

https://www.geekwire.com/2021/amazon-worker-union-leader-alabama-vote-breathed-new-life-labor-movement/

*

AMAZON'S "POWER HOUR"

"What Amazon Does to Poor Cities" (*The Atlantic*/ Alana Semuels)

(power hour prize – a cookie)

https://www.theatlantic.com/business/archive/2018/02/amazon-warehouses-poor-cities/552020/

"Amazon warehouse employees speak out about the 'brutal' reality of working during the holidays, when 60-hour weeks are mandatory and ambulance calls are common" (*Business Insider*/Isobel Asher Hamilton and Áine Cain

https://www.businessinsider.com/amazon-employees-describe-peak-2019-2

*

WAREHOUSES

"Mapping Amazon – Where the Online Giant Locates Its Warehouses and Why" (Good Jobs First)
https://storymaps.arcgis.com/stories/adc5ff253a3643f88d39e7f3ef1a09ee

Warehouses: Last Week Tonight with John Oliver

https://youtu.be/d9m7d07k22A ("Power hour" @ 12:02)

*

INSUFFICIENT TRAINING

"Working At Amazon (Mice, Unpaid Wages, Mandatory Overtime)" (Youtuber Cedric Johnson, 48.9K followers)(info on training @ 5:02)

https://youtu.be/WBarm4TMZyY

"What the hell are they teaching to the new hires?"

https://imgur.com/eeDvxAE

Employee reviews / Indeed

https://www.indeed.com/cmp/Amazon.com/reviews?fjobti-tle=Warehouse+Worker

Employee reviews / Glassdoor

https://www.glassdoor.com/Reviews/Amazon-Reviews-E6036.htm?filter.iso3Language=eng (sorted by 'popular')

*

BETTER TRAINING

"What would you suggest Amazon.com management do to prevent others from leaving?" (*Indeed.com*)

https://www.indeed.com/cmp/Amazon.com/faq/what-would-you-suggest-amazon-com-management-do-to-prevent-others-from-leaving

*

SAFETY TRAINING

"How Amazon hid its safety crisis" (*RevealNews*/Will Evans)

https://revealnews.org/article/how-amazon-hid-its-safety-crisis/

"You're Just Disposable": Former Amazon Workers Speak Out | "Amazon Empire" | FRONTLINE

https://youtu.be/3-KMXng5Cp0

*

WORKERS' CONDITIONS – SAFETY

Amazon Employees Speak Out About Workplace Conditions | *NBC Nightly News*

https://youtu.be/tvdyxXhVNRE critical

National COSH Announces "Dirty Dozen" Employers

(2018) https://coshnetwork.org/national-cosh-announces-%E2%80%9Cdirty-dozen%E2%80%9D-employers

(2019) https://coshnetwork.org/2019-Dirty-Dozen-Release

(2020) https://coshnetwork.org/2020-04-23_National_COSH_Announces_2020_Dirty_Dozen_Report

(Dishonorable Mention)

*

COVID

"Leaked Amazon Memo Details Plan to Smear Fired Warehouse Organizer: 'He's Not Smart or Articulate'" (*VICE News*/Paul Blest)

https://www.vice.com/en/article/5dm8bx/leaked-amazon-memo-details-plan-to-smear-fired-warehouse-organizer-hes-not-smart-or-articulate

"Gaps in Amazon's Response as Virus Spreads to More Than 50 Warehouse" (New York Times/Karen Weise and Kate Conger)

https://www.nytimes.com/2020/04/05/technology/coronavirus-amazon-workers.html

"Amazon employees say safety measures not enforced at local facilities" (*WSOC TV: WSOC-TV Channel 9*)

https://youtu.be/e-PDcRWq9Oc

*

DISTANCE ASSISTANTS

Amazon deploys AI 'distance assistants' to notify warehouse workers if they get too close

https://www.theverge.com/2020/6/16/21292669/social-distancing-amazon-ai-assistant-warehouses-covid-19

*

CHAOS DURING THE EARLY WEEKS OF THE PANDEMIC

"Rumors, death, and a tech overhaul: Inside Amazon's race to hire 175,000 workers during a pandemic" (*MIT Technology Review*/Hayden Field)

https://www.technologyreview.com/2020/06/12/1003360/inside-amazons-pandemic-hiring-race/

Amazon's Big Breakdown (The New York Times/John Herman

https://www.nytimes.com/interactive/2020/05/27/magazine/amazon-coronavirus.html

"Frustrated Amazon shoppers vent at record levels" (*The Washington Post*/Jay Greene)

https://www.washingtonpost.com/technology/2020/05/21/amazon-shopper-complaints/

*

GLITCHES

"Amazon Just had a Worst-Case-Scenario Moment for the Second Year in a Row. Here's Why It's a Big Deal" (*Inc.com*/Jason Aten)

https://www.inc.com/jason-aten/amazon-just-had-a-worst-case-scenario-prime-day-for-second-year-in-a-row-heres-why-its-a-big-deal.html

"Amazon customers complained about technical difficulties for the 2nd Prime Day in a row" (*Business Insider*/Kate Taylor)

https://www.businessinsider.com/amazon-website-glitches-on-prime-day-2019-7

"Amazon Says Error Removed Listings" (*The New York Times*/Motoko Rich)

https://www.nytimes.com/2009/04/14/technology/internet/14amazon.html

"Despite the Glitches, Shoppers Can't Quit Amazon" (*The Atlantic*/Alana Semuels)

https://www.theatlantic.com/technology/archive/2018/07/prime-day-amazon-website/565412/

"Amazon says the Kindle Paperwhite will get new firmware" (*Good-EReader*/Michael Kozlowski)

https://goodereader.com/blog/kindle/amazon-says-the-kindle-paperwhite-3-will-get-new-firmware

"Amazon sends accidental gift email to shoppers due to glitch" (*Reuters*/Jeffrey Dastin)

https://www.reuters.com/article/us-amazon-com-glitch/amazon-sends-accidental-gift-email-to-shoppers-due-to-glitch-idUSKCN1BV01F 2020

*

<u>ISSUES WITH GETTING PAID</u>

"Missing wages, grueling shifts, and bottles of urine: The disturbing accounts of Amazon delivery drivers may reveal the true human cost of 'free' shipping" (*Business Insider*/Hayley Peterson)

https://www.businessinsider.com/amazon-delivery-drivers-reveal-claims-of-disturbing-work-conditions-2018-8

"'Amazon is not taking care of us': Warehouse workers say they're struggling to get paid despite sick leave policy" (*CNBC*/Annie Palmer) https://www.cnbc.com/2020/04/08/amazon-warehouse-workers-say-they-struggle-to-get-paid-despite-sick-leave-policy.html

"Amazon Delivery Drivers in California Sue Over Unpaid Wages" (Bloomberg Law/Kathleen Dailey)

https://news.bloomberglaw.com/daily-labor-report/amazon-delivery-drivers-in-california-sue-over-unpaid-wages

"Amazon warehouse workers in Chicago say the company cheated them of overtime hours" (*Recode*/Shirin Ghaffary)

https://www.vox.com/recode/2019/7/26/8931013/amazon-prime-day-workers-chicago-cheated-overtime-hours-workers-amazonians-united-prime-week

"Class Action: Amazon Owes Unpaid Wages for Sending New Hires Home Early Due to 'E-Verify' System Error" (*ClassAction.org*/Corrado Rizzi))

https://www.classaction.org/news/class-action-amazon-owes-unpaid-wages-for-sending-new-hires-home-early-due-to-e-verify-system-error

"Amazon will pay $61.7 million to settle claims it withheld tips from delivery workers" (*CNBC*/Annie Palmer)

https://www.cnbc.com/2021/02/02/amazon-to-pay-61point7-million-in-ftc-driver-tipping-settlement-.html

"Amazon kept $62 million in tips intended for drivers, FTC says" (CBS NEWS/Irina Ivanova) https://www.cbsnews.com/news/amazon-flex-62-million-tips-delivery-drivers/

*

SHIPPING

"Amazon will spend nearly $1.5B in Q4 for one-day delivery initiative as shipping costs skyrocket" (*Geekwire*/Taylor Soper)

https://www.geekwire.com/2019/amazon-will-spend-nearly-1-5b-q4-one-day-delivery-initiative-shipping-costs-skyrocket/

"The Cost of Next-Day Delivery" (*Buzzfeed News*/Caroline O'Donovan and Ken Bensinger)

https://www.buzzfeednews.com/article/carolineodonovan/amazon-next-day-delivery-deaths

"Amazon Makes It Harder for Sellers to Avoid Shipping Service" (Bloomberg/Spencer Soper)

https://www.bloomberg.com/news/articles/2020-08-18/amazon-makes-it-harder-for-sellers-to-avoid-its-shipping-service

*

JIFFIES & RECYCLING

Why Amazon's new streamlined packaging is jamming up recycling centers

https://www.washingtonpost.com/technology/2019/02/11/why-amazons-new-streamlined-packaging-is-jamming-up-recycling-centers/

"How to recycle Amazon packaging (yes, all of it)" (*Mashable*/Siobhan Neela-Stock)

https://mashable.com/article/how-to-recycle-amazon-packaging/

"List of mergers and acquisitions by Amazon" (*Wikipedia*)

https://en.wikipedia.org/wiki/List_of_mergers_and_acquisitions_by_Amazon

*

TAX INCENTIVES

"On Amazon's Time" (*Gizmodo*/Bryan Menegus)

https://gizmodo.com/on-amazon-s-time-1826570882

"Tracking Subsidies, Promoting Accountability in Economic Development – Amazon Tracker" (*Good Jobs First*) https://www.goodjobsfirst.org/amazon-tracker

"$48K per new job? New York tax incentives for Amazon HQ2 site stir concerns" (*Syracuse.com/The Washington Post*)

https://www.syracuse.com/state/2018/11/amazon_hq2_ny_tax_incentives_concerns.html

"Tax incentives are good for Amazon. What about the local economy?" (*Chicago Tribune*/Lauren Zumbach)

https://www.chicagotribune.com/business/ct-biz-amazon-warehouse-jobs-0311-story.html

"Nashville approves $17.5M Amazon incentive" (*The Tennesean*/Yihyun Jeong)

https://www.tennessean.com/story/news/2019/03/19/nashville-metro-council-approves-17-5-m-amazon-incentive/3212031002/

"Amazon gets $7.5 million in tax credits for Wisconsin projects as Triad awaits details on its own" (*Triad Business Journal*/Rich Kirchen)

https://www.bizjournals.com/triad/news/2019/03/26/amazon-gets-7-5-million-in-tax-credits-for.html

*

HQ2

"Amazon HQ2 and NYC: A timeline of the botched deal" (*Curbed NY*/Amy Plitt)

https://ny.curbed.com/2019/2/18/18226681/amazon-hq2-new-york-city-timeline

"Amazon's HQ2 Spectacle Isn't Just Shameful—It Should Be Illegal" (*The Atlantic*/Derek Thompson)

https://www.theatlantic.com/ideas/archive/2018/11/amazons-hq2-spectacle-should-be-illegal/575539/

"New York offered Amazon nearly $1 billion more in tax credits than previously known for its HQ2 deal" (*Business Insider*/Weng Cheong)

https://www.businessinsider.com/ny-amazon-hq2-nearly-1-billion-more-than-known-for-2020-1

*

UNDERCOVER OPERATIONS

"After undercover sting, Amazon files suit against 1,000 Fiverr users over fake product reviews" (Geekwire/Jacob Demmitt)

https://www.geekwire.com/2015/after-conducting-undercover-sting-amazon-files-suit-against-1000-fiverr-users-over-fake-product-reviews/

"Secret Amazon Reports Expose the Company's Surveillance of Labor and Environmental Groups" (*VICE Magazine*/Lauren Kaori Gurley)

https://www.vice.com/en/article/5dp3yn/amazon-leaked-reports-expose-spying-warehouse-workers-labor-union-environmental-groups-social-movements

*

50 POUNDS PACKAGES

"Exercise with facemask; Are we handling a devil's sword?" – A physiological hypothesis (*US National Library of Medicine National Institutes of Health*/Baskaran Chandrasekaran? and Shifra Fernandes)

https://www.ncbi.nlm.nih.gov/pmc/articles/PMC7306735/

"Hate lugging cat litter? Don't make us Amazon warehouse workers do it" (*The Guardian*/Anonymous)

https://www.theguardian.com/us-news/2018/dec/05/hate-lugging-cat-litter-dont-make-us-amazon-warehouse-workers-do-it

*

AMAZON EMPLOYEES

Number of Amazon.com employees from 2007 to 2019 (*Statista*)

https://www.statista.com/statistics/234488/number-of-amazon-employees/

The Former And Current Employees (FACE) of Amazon

https://sites.google.com/site/thefaceofamazon/ & https://sites.google.com/site/thefaceofamazon/home/media-coverage

Criticism of Amazon (*Wikipedia*)

https://en.wikipedia.org/wiki/Criticism_of_Amazon

*

WAGES – TODAY ONLY 1.9 PERCENT OF HOURLY WORKERS MAKE THE FEDERAL MINIMUM WAGE

"Minimum wage in America: How many people are earning $7.25 an hour?" (*USA Facts*)

https://usafacts.org/articles/minimum-wage-america-how-many-people-are-earning-725-hour/

"Krystal and Rachel: Amazon And Walmart STIFF Workers As They Rake In Billions" (*Youtube The Hill* 1.8 M subscribers)

https://youtu.be/TLCBQB3lEDA

*

TRACKING SUBSIDIES

"Subsidies Awarded to Amazon: at least $3,757,000,000... and Counting!" (*Good Jobs First*)

https://www.goodjobsfirst.org/amazon-tracker

*

WORLD DOMINATION

"How Jeff Bezos Is Hurtling Toward World Domination" (*Newsweek*/Alexander Nazaryan)

https://www.newsweek.com/2016/07/22/jeff-bezos-amazon-ceo-world-domination-479508.html

"How Amazon Destroys the Intellectual Justifications for Capitalism" (*Current Affairs*/Nathan J. Robinson)

https://www.currentaffairs.org/2020/12/how-amazon-destroys-the-intellectual-justifications-for-capitalism

Amazon Empire: The Rise and Reign of Jeff Bezos (full film) | FRONTLINE

https://youtu.be/RVVfJVj5z8s

*

ABOUT THE AUTHOR

I was born in Vienna, Austria, but I don't ski, yodel or play an instrument. And, even though it's one of the most famous musical drama movies, I watched the "Sound of Music" with Julie Andrews only after I found out that all my American friends had seen the movie. At least, I show off my roots by watching the Vienna New Year's Concert (Neujahrskonzert) and the famed Hahnenkamm downhill, religiously.

To be honest, I'd rather be a world-citizen. These days pretty much everything we do affects people elsewhere. I feel very fortunate to have had so many amazing experiences on my travels around the world.

Never shying away from insane work, I analyzed 100,000+ emails for effectiveness and personal appeal to devise a method to write best emails. After all, writing best emails is the most effective way to reach customers and influencers. I also dug through thousands of online reviews to find out how to get them and how they can help to boost sales. My work has been featured on *Bloomberg*, in *SUCCESS*, and in *Entrepreneur*.

If I have found one truth in life, then it is:

"Go for it! Do the work because it will pay off, enjoy the moment because it might not last!"

*

Gisela Hausmann is a proud mother of two and grandmother of one. She lives with her two cats, Artemis and Yin-Yang, in Greenville, SC.

Gisela's website: http://www.giselahausmann.com/

Follow her at https://twitter.com/Naked_Determina

MORE BOOKS

About writing best emails:

NAKED WORDS 2.0: The Effective 157-Word Email

NAKED TEXT Email Writing Skills for Teenagers

73 Ways to Turn a Me-Mail Into an E-mail

*

Inspirational

Naked Eye-Opener: To Reach the Dream You Must Forget About It

Naked Determination: 41 Stories About Overcoming Fear

*

Books for indie authors:

Naked News for Indie Authors How NOT to Invest Your Marketing $$$

Naked Truths About Getting Book Reviews 2018

Naked Good Reads: How to find Readers

3 Little Blue Books for Authors [53 Dos & Don'ts Nobody Is Telling You ? 101 Clues to Get More Out of Facebook ? Essential Manners for the Modern Author]

BOOK MARKETING: The Funnel Factor: Including 100 Media Pitches (paperback only)

BAT SHIT CRAZY Review Requests: Email Humor

* * *

*

Made in the USA
Las Vegas, NV
31 August 2021

29200995R00068